Traffic-free family & leisure cycling in
Kent, Sussex, Surrey & Hampshire

Cycling Days Out

South East England

Deirdre Huston

Cycling
Days Out
South East England

ISBN 978-1-906148-24-9

Front cover photo: Viking Coastal Trail.
Back cover photos: *Top left* Richmond Park, *Top right* Thames Path, *Bottom* Deers Leap.

Photography by **Deirdre Huston**

 All maps reproduced by permission of Ordnance Survey on behalf of The Controller of Her Majesty's Stationery Office. © Crown Copyright. 100025218

Alice Holt Forest, Bedgebury Forest & Friston Forest trail maps reproduced by kind permission from the Forestry Commission.

 Design & production by **Jane Beagley**
Edited by **John Coefield**
www.v-publishing.co.uk

MIX
Paper from responsible sources
FSC® C112556

contents

cycle routes at a glance

THE IDEA FOR THIS BOOK BEGAN WITH TWO OBSERVATIONS:

Firstly, I noticed how much friends and family enjoyed traffic-free cycling on cycleways such as the Downs Link and I wondered what other prime, traffic-free cycling I could find in the south east. My efforts were well rewarded! Kent, Sussex, Surrey and Hampshire are brimming over with cycling opportunities.

Secondly, my family and I rode the The Sunshine Trail on the Isle of Wight and I thought about how cycling is the perfect way to explore new locations – whether it's on a day out or a weekend away. It's free, healthy, environmentally-friendly and it enables you to see and experience places in a whole new way.

I have lived in the south east all my life and yet I was still stunned by the beauty and character of the 'hidden' landscape that I discovered while researching these trails. I cycled along trails which offered beauty and interest in so many different ways: vistas and tiny details, windswept coasts and sun filtered by forest leaves, old railway tracks and rivers steeped in history, wildlife crossing my path when I least expected it and the British seaside at its best. Cycling enabled me to see familiar locations such as Hampton Court with new eyes. How else could you have a day out in London that costs nothing but shows you a side to our capital which is often missed, even by locals? The south east may be densely populated but it is still possible to experience a feeling of 'wilderness' and the power of nature if you set out on two wheels.

There's a wide selection of forests, cycleways, country parks and tourist trails on offer in this guide. Each has been selected because they can give somebody a brilliant day out and the guide's first job is to help you select the type of traffic-free cycling that you hanker after on any given day. Take your pick: short or long trails, cycling or mountain biking, linear or loop, family rides or romantic getaways, trees or sea, fields or canal, flat or hilly, smooth or bumpy? The choice is yours.

I thought about how much it would help to have information easily at hand when you're planning or ready to go. Bike hire? Stop for food? We give you plenty of ideas and refer you to websites to save you time going round in circles online.

The route directions, maps, information on 'easy access', food, drink, parking and bike hire are all there to help you plan your ride so that you can relax and enjoy your cycling. Want to know which part of a cycleway is more family-friendly? The route details should help. Teenagers think flat rides are boring? Try mountain biking. Need to find a place to stay? Take a look at the accommodation we've spotted during our research. Have somebody in your party who rides an adapted or hand cycle? Check the easy access pointers.

Choose the trail which matches your wishlist for a bike ride on any particular day and you're more or less guaranteed a day to remember. Whether you like your days out to be relaxing, exhilarating, physically demanding or gentle on the legs, there should be some beautiful traffic-free cycling here for you.

There's some beautiful places just waiting to be discovered! I know that I shall return to many of them time after time.

Happy cycling!
Deirdre

ACKNOWLEDGEMENTS

When I looked back on my year, I was struck by images flashing through my mind of all the stunning days out I'd enjoyed while researching this guidebook. It was a privilege to share the experience with a number of family and friends who inspired me to see each place with fresh new eyes and enthusiasm. We circled round vicious dogs, fixed punctures, did without the lazy sun-bathing to cycle, honing our ability to spot good cafés and pubs while racing over unexpected bumps and ditches to always (well almost always...) make it back in time.

Love and thanks to Bev (fellow expert on easy cycling and cafés), Carol (encouragement and making me cycle fast), Debbie (help and understanding on the niceties of easy access), Julie (willing to go anywhere), Liz (trusting me with a rare day off), RJH (Medway insights), Rory (always up for it), Sarah (no hill is too big), Sean (how close can you ride your bike to my camera?), Tegan (the best day out ever) and Ian (words can't say thanks enough for all your help and encouragement).

Thanks also to staff at the Forestry Commission, Sustrans and CTC (now Cycling UK) for their help, information and the services which they provide to cyclists in general.

HOW TO USE THIS BOOK

This book is all about having a fun day out on your bike with your family or friends. I've tried to make the planning of a trip as easy as possible, by providing lots of useful info on places to eat, drink and stay.

We've divided the cycling into four main categories, with some routes and trails being covered by more than one category.

FORESTS

There's something primeval about the way the human psyche reacts to forest and woodland: it relaxes and invigorates us. The Forestry Commission provides many cycle tracks in 'working forests' around the country. Experience the forest environment whilst staying within easy reach of facilities or venture into remote muddy corners. Each forest offers something different!

CYCLEWAYS

These well-trodden canal towpaths and old railway lines are finding fresh use in the new Millenium. Why? Because they tend to be flat, reasonably surfaced and great for easy off-road cycling. A third type of cycleway is opening up the countryside: vital new paths, accessible to all, often funded by charities such as Sustrans.

TOURIST TRAILS

There's a 'holiday' feel to these trails, which might make you want to get on your bike. They offer the chance for locals and tourists to explore places where cars can't go! Circuits include old bridleways, new cycleways and may be linked by quiet lanes. Landscapes vary from coastal to down land. A couple of the routes require mountain bikes.

COUNTRY PARKS

These parks have one thing in common: traffic-free cycling! This eclectic mix varies from town to coast, from 'Royal' parks to a reservoir, from a rural 'biking' education centre to a RSPB reserve on the banks of the industrial Thames. Each park will suit very different cyclists. Take your pick!

KEY

ROUTE GRADES/DIFFICULTY LEVELS
(difficulty level not connected to length of route)

*	Mainly flat and firm-surfaced tracks, or concrete/tarmac.
**	Includes some gradients on hard surfaces, or some flat cycling on off-road surfaces.
***	Includes some gradients on off-road surfaces or a significant amount of climbing on hard surfaces.
****	Includes some gradients on surfaces such as sand or deep mud, which may be very hard-going. Some hills may be steep or particularly long.

MAP KEY

Most of our routes in this book are shown on Ordnance Survey 1:50,000 scale mapping. An OS map legend can be downloaded for free from *www.ordnancesurvey.co.uk*

A couple of routes are shown on Forestry Commission mapping, reproduced with their kind permission. These routes are also waymarked on the ground. Here's a guide to some of the symbols we use on the maps and in the directions.

 The **main route**.

 An **optional route**, shortcut or diversion. Optional diversions are also highlighted in grey text in the directions.

 Sections of trail particularly suitable for **easy access**: off-road wheelchairs, buggies and hand cycles.

S Indicates the **start** of the ride/route.

2 **Direction** markers.

>< Indicates an **optional route**, a **shortcut** or an **interesting diversion** to a pub or café. Optional diversions are also highlighted in grey text in the directions.

33 Used only on a couple of routes (both in the New Forest), these relate to actual numbered **forest waymarkers** which aid navigation in the middle of these big forests.

L – Left   **R** – Right   **SA** – Straight ahead

EASY ACCESS

We have flagged up trails or, more precisely, sections of trails which may be of interest to adventurous hand-cyclists/wheelchair users/parents with buggies. Reading the route description should give you a good idea of the trail surface and gradients but this description is primarily aimed at cyclists on two-wheeled, foot-pedalled bikes and may not mention all changes in surface and those small slopes which can be an unfortunate feature of access points. These can be a particular pain if you are alone so when trying a trail for the first time, you are strongly advised to take along a friend.

In terms of 'easy access', the description can only provide a broad guide as there are so many different variables. It should ideally be used as a starting point. You know what terrain your hand cycle/wheelchair/buggy is suited to. Where possible, we have provided links and you are strongly advised to research more information.

Having said that, there's some beautiful wild places out there and one of the benefits of some well-designed and well-maintained cycleways is that they make them accessible to more people. Enjoy!

For more detailed independent information visit *www.disabledgo.com*

Cycling For All

For inclusive cycling sessions across London, see *http://cyclingforall.org*

For information on locations where inclusive cycling is available across the South East, see *www.cyclinguk.org/ride/inclusive-cycling*

A NOTE ABOUT WEBSITES

Where possible, I've included useful websites that give extra visitor information on different trails and country parks, or provide handy downloadable PDF guides and maps. In some instances, where the website addresses are very long, we've shrunk them down using 'tinyurl'. When you enter a tinyurl it will take you to the actual website which will very likely have a BIG web address! Just be sure to add the 'http://' before the address to make sure it works, for example: *http://tinyurl.com/NewForestPodcasts*

USEFUL WEBSITES

Sustrans

The UK's leading sustainable transport charity.
www.sustrans.org.uk

Cycling UK (formerly CTC)

A not-for-profit organisation, Cycling UK protects and promotes the rights of cyclists in the UK.
www.cyclinguk.org

Explore Kent

Find out more about cycling and country parks in Kent, including easy access information.
www.kent.gov.uk/explorekent

Enjoy England

Find out more about the Cyclists Welcome scheme. Handy if booking accommodation.
http://tinyurl.com/cyclistswelcome

BIKE RACKS

Fitting three, four or five bikes in and onto a car is always going to be a bit of a jigsaw puzzle. A well-designed bike rack helps. It doesn't have to be expensive but it's worth remembering that the first couple of times you use it, it will take longer and appear more fiddly. Once you've worked out the best way for your particular set of bikes to fit on board your car, the whole process should be quicker and easier the next time.

Detachable racks can be fine although they are less secure if you want to leave bikes unattended. Racks which fix to a tow-bar probably leave less scope for human error and avoid the high lifting which roof bike racks demand. Some people take the wheels off and squash all the bikes into their boot but many families don't have that option. Find a way that works and it will open up a whole range of cycling opportunities, with many places to ride and explore.

FAMILY RIDING

There are over 20 'days out' in this guide which could be brilliant for a family. Some may be better suited to families with older children and others are ideal for a young family but might bore teenagers. Read this section for added tips on suitability for kids and combine with information in the route directions to decide if the trail is right for your family.

The sign at one trail centre reads...

Take nothing but pictures...
Leave nothing but footprints...
Kill nothing but time...

LONDON BIKE HIRE

London Cycle Hire Scheme

The London Cycle Hire Scheme is based in central London (roughly Zone 1 on a Tube map) and so, geographically, is not directly relevant to our London routes. If, however, you are interested in exploring Hyde Park, Kensington Gardens or Regents Park, look out for the bike hire stations in these parks. The bike hire stations are self-service and there's no need to book, but you can register for 24 hour, quicker access. You must pay an access fee (for example £2 for 24 hours) and a usage charge (for example up to an hour £2, and for example, every 30 minutes thereafter might be another £2). For longer periods of hire, greater flexibility and a wider variety of bike models you may prefer to use a bike hire company. Full details are available on the website.
https://tfl.gov.uk/modes/cycling/santander-cycles

Action Bikes SW1

Hires out the classic folder: the Brompton L6. Includes lock, lights, helmet and rain cover. 'Try before you buy' scheme. Also at Embankment, Wimbledon and Staines.
T 0207 799 2233
E info@actionbikes.co.uk
www.actionbikes.co.uk

Cycling For All

Cycling For All is a London-wide network funded by Sport England to increase cycling opportunities for people of all ages and abilities. They offer regular inclusive cycling opportunities across London and may also provide outreach sessions for community events.
http://cyclingforall.org

An hour's train journey from London, explore the South Downs National Park with Hasssocks Community Cycle Hire.
www.hassockscommunitycyclehire.com

City Bike Service EC2A 3EN

7-speed hybrid cycles. Lock, lights and cycle map of Central/East London included in hire. Try out commuting, or explore the East End of London (Docklands, Lee Valley Park, Olympic site, Greenwich, Thames Barrier...) by bicycle. Regent Canal, River Lee and Thames cycle routes are within easy distance.
T 0207 702 9999
www.citybikeservice.co.uk

Go Pedal!

Bikes delivered and collected to most areas of London. Includes helmet and lock. Best for visitors wanting to explore London on funky, comfortable and practical bikes
T 07850 796 320
E info@gopedal.co.uk
www.gopedal.co.uk

London Bicycle Tour Company SE1 9PP

Bikes: hybrids, mountain bikes and traditional style. Tandems also available. Central location, with maps and route advice. Good for families – a limited selection of children's equipment is available for use for free, if a cycle is rented by an adult. They specialise in **bicycle tours** – great for those who want to gain confidence.
T 0207 928 6838
E mail@londonbicycle.com
www.londonbicycle.com

London Recumbents SE21

Sell a wide range of specialist bikes for families and special needs users, as well as many recumbents in Dulwich Park and hire bicycles for families, children and people with special needs in Dulwich Park and Battersea Park, London.

T 0208 299 6636
E info@londonrecumbents.com
www.londonrecumbents.com

On Your Bike SE1

Good for exploring the Thames Cycle Path eastbound, and the canals north of the river.

T 0207 378 6669
E bikehire@onyourbike.com
www.onyourbike.com

Smith Brothers SW19

Hybrids for hire – good for those living in or visiting southwest London who wish to explore Wimbledon Common, Richmond Park, or the river Wandle.

T 0208 946 2270

Velorution – Rent a Folder W1W 8BD

Folding bikes, delivery & collection to/from accommodation included. Convenient and flexible, folding bikes can go on the tube or be left at the cloakroom.

T 0207 637 4004
E info@velorution.biz
www.velorution.biz

kent

kent

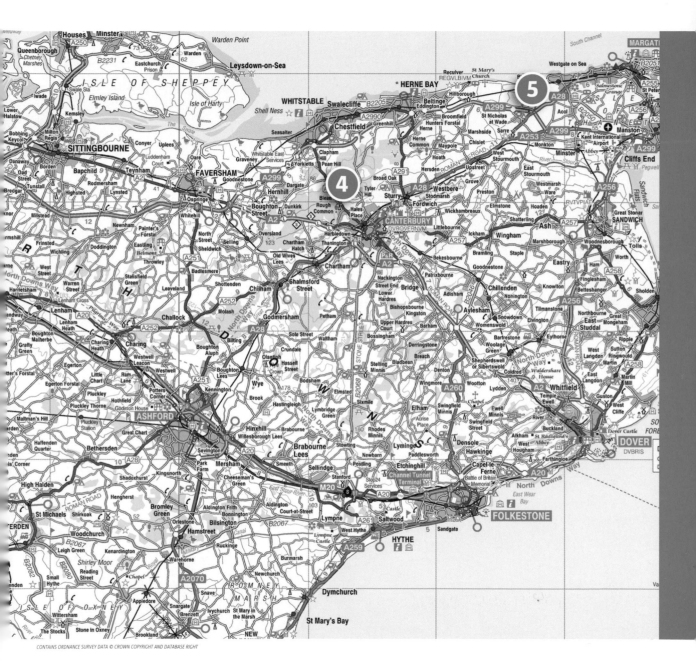

1 BEWL WATER LOOP

COUNTRY PARK

GRADE: ✳ ✳ / ✳ ✳ ✳

DISTANCE: 20km / 12.5 miles

MAPS: OS Explorer 136

Cycle route open May – October

This stunning reservoir is the largest lake in southeast England and offers breathtaking cycling. You can choose a simple linear route to a nearby pub, or follow the challenging 12.5 mile Round Reservoir route. Light plays on the water, fishermen wait for fish and sailing boats wait for the wind. And cyclists? They pedal...

The Round Reservoir route will reward your efforts with cycling tracks that are unpredictable enough to keep you on your toes, and hills that stop at just the right time. The intricate shoreline of Bewl Water awaits you. If you're up to it, you won't be disappointed.

Some people take a picnic and linger to enjoy the inlets and wooded backdrop while others like to complete the whole loop before recharging. We've added in a simple diversion to the local pub if you fancy a swift pint too.

Cycling at Bewl is guaranteed to soothe away the irritations of the modern world. If you can, put your mobile phone on silent and soak up the ambience. You won't regret it.

LINKS WITH
Bedgebury Forest is on the other side of the A21.

EASY ACCESS
Despite hard surfaces the gradients could be a problem for some. See accessibility section on Bewl Water's website (*www.bewlwater.co.uk*). A wheelchair accessible fishing boat is available for fly fishing (**T** 01892 890 352) and Mariners of Bewl is an integrated sailing club for the physically disabled and able bodied (*www.mariners-of-bewl.org.uk*).

PUBLIC TRANSPORT
TRAIN STATION: **Wadhurst**

PARKING
Approx. £8 per car (may vary for special events). Pass the Outdoor Centre and bear right up the hill to the Visitor Centre car park.

BIKE HIRE
BEWL BIKE HIRE
T 01892 891 446
www.bewlbikehire.com

FOOD, DRINK AND ACCOMMODATION
THE BULL INN, THREE LEG CROSS
Reputed to be one of the oldest dwelling places in the country. Real ales, pleasant garden and four ensuite B&B rooms. Popular with walkers, cyclists and fishermen.
T 01580 200 586
www.thebullinn.co.uk

BEWL WATER CAFÉ
The café is clean, serves simple but freshly-prepared food and has a fantastic outlook over the reservoir.

POINTS OF INTEREST
BEWL WATER
Bewl Water offers all the right elements for peace and tranquility: water, Wealden woods and grassy banks. And it's easily accessible from the A21. Recent updates to activities include a sandy beach (where exhausted cyclists could collapse?), hydro-balling (!), children's fishing and model boating. Then of course, there's traditional fishing and watersports. Facilities include: Visitor Centre, toilets, café and shop. Open daily in summer, 10.30am – 5.30pm, and winter weekends, 11am – 4.30pm. **Note the cycle route is only open May to October.** Check out the website for up to date information
www.bewlwater.co.uk

FAMILY RIDING
No easy cycling, but see the linear route for families on p23. The climbing on the Round Reservoir route would be too much for most kids given the length of the route.

ROUND RESERVOIR ROUTE

You would be well advised to cycle the hardest, if arguably the most enjoyable, part of the trail first.

S Turn **L** out of the car park. Follow the *Round Bewl* white bicycle signs towards the exit. Turn **L** at the top of the slope. Pass the clinking sailing boats, cycle through the open gates at the exit and take the clearly-marked track **L**, round the metal barrier.

2 At the top of the hill, take a **L** into Hook Hill Lane, following the brown signs. Follow the lane round and down, ignoring any turn-offs into private houses on your left. Enjoy the steep downhill but watch out for the gate at the bottom.

3 After the gate, follow the muddy track **R** through the woods. You are riding along the banks of Bewl Water. In spring, the scent and tint of bluebells is unmissable.

Come to an open stretch with views opening up onto Bewl in all its glory. Ducks quack and boats are tied in lines, ready for fishermen. This is fantastic, medium-level off-road cycling with satisfying ups and downs on bumpy mud tracks. And all the while, the water glitters through the trees or laps the grassy banks. There are strategically-placed benches if you want to linger, and you probably will. You could be a million miles from civilisation, especially if you're here on a weekday.

By the wooden fence, ignore the fork to the right and keep **SA**. Follow the unmarked track around the banks of Bewl Water. Stay on the lakeside or follow the trail as it twists right into dense woodland only to re-emerge moments later. Climb the short, bumpy steep ascent right back onto a wide mud track. Follow it **L** through the woods and along the undulating open bank. Look out for reflections on the water.

There are some steep little ups and downs as the path meanders through woods. Two low-lying railway sleepers cross the path (a bike-calming measure?). Cycle on **SA**, sweeping up and down. Follow the track away from the bank, riding briefly with fields on your right. Butterflies flutter across your path, and rustles in the wood suggest more wildlife may be close at hand. The path meanders on with some sharp turns, passing inlets, trees and open stretches.

Cycle on. Upon reaching a wooden waymarker (brown Bewl Water leisure sign), turn **R** through the wooden gate. Ride (or push!) your bike up the steep track. Head **L**, following the track. Cycle **R**, following the wooden bridleway waymarker. Reach a metalled lane. Follow the brown Bewl Water route sign **SA**.

4 At the top of the hill, follow the brown Bewl Water sign **R**. Cycle past the lane to Chessons Farm. Look out for beautiful views across the Weald towards the oast house and a church spire.

Take a **L** up the lane towards Birchett's Green, following the brown Bewl Water sign. Enjoy fantastic sweeping downhills with the wind wrapping around your ears. Hold that sensation as you climb the inevitable up that follows. Pass Birchetts Point on your left. These lanes tend to be very quiet but you are now on public roads and will meet the odd car. Pace yourself: this is a hilly stretch of tarmac. Pass Quarry Hill on your right and keep pedalling! Climb to the red brick and tile houses at the top of Birchett's Green Lane.

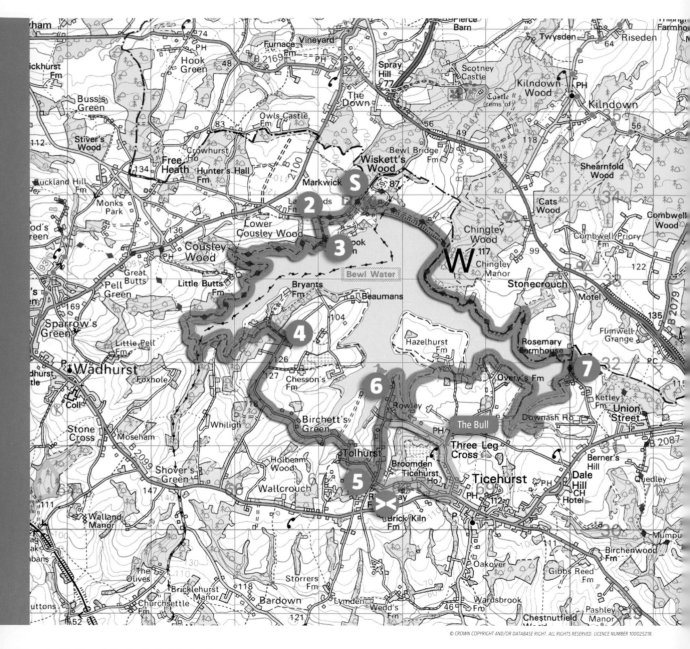

© CROWN COPYRIGHT AND/OR DATABASE RIGHT. ALL RIGHTS RESERVED. LICENCE NUMBER 100025218.

5 Here you have a choice. Continue on the Round Bewl Route, turning **L**, following the brown Bewl Water sign. Ride on until you reach a small crossroads with a gate on your left. Ride **SA**, following the brown Bewl sign.

Look out for Bewl Water on your left.

✕ OPTIONAL ROUTE

Or, if you wish to go on a very small diversion to the pub, turn **R** and then immediately **L** into Vineyard Lane. The lane climbs and winds. Towards the top, you pass a big cream mansion on your right and a pond on your left. Reach Ticehurst. Go **L** at the main road (B2099) for a very short distance. Turn **L** again almost immediately into Cross Lane and coast down the hill. At the bottom of the lane, you will see The Bull pub. Turn **L** and climb Borders Lane. At the top, rejoin the main Round Bewl Route, following the brown sign **R**.

6 Go through the wooden gate marked *Bewl Water*. Soon, you pass through another wooden gate marked *Nature Reserve*. It's good to be back off-road and beside Bewl Water. Ride on.

After a small, flat wooden bridge, watch out for the raised sleeper across the stony track as you head up towards the wooden gate. Follow the white bike sign **SA** through the gate, leaving the Nature Reserve. Ride along the narrow bridleway as it leads you around to the front of the house. See distant barns and a 'members only' car park. Follow the track and wooden bridleway waymarker **SA**. Bump your way down the sleepers and stones to go through another gate. Go around the metal barrier and across the track. Turn **L**, following the wooden bridleway sign. Pass Dunsters Bay car park, relax and follow the winding mud trail as it leads you round the southern contours of Bewl Water. Pass through a wooden gate.

7 Ride **L** over the bridge across the reservoir. Turn **L** through an open wooden gate and follow the muddy track (in the direction of the public footpath sign). Pass through a narrow gateway. Follow the mud track round the banks of Bewl. See the oast house in the distance on the far bank. The path becomes a wider track through the woods. Ride the steep drop to the bridge. This path is do-able by all but there's enough bumps, ups, downs and curves to make it fun for those who want to ride a bit faster, giving due consideration to other path users.

The path widens and becomes level conglomerate. This is now ideal for easy riding, baby carriages and so on. See the Visitor Centre and Sailing Centre across the water to your left. Ride beyond the dam and cycle **L**, taking the lower path behind the dam. This is a steep descent on a stony path. Bear **L** where the path joins a lane. Keep it steady up the hill. Pass through the gate. Turn **R** and then **L** to return to the Visitor Centre. One last small slope to climb before you reach refreshments and your car.

LINEAR ROUTE FOR FAMILIES

The most family-friendly part of the circuit is the last section so I would suggest doing this route in reverse, i.e. ride **R** and then **L** out of the car park, heading down towards Bewl Water. Follow the path behind the dam. Cycle along the Round Bewl Trail as it winds around the banks of Bewl Water. After some time, pass some barns and a private car park on your right. Here the bridleway turns **R** behind a house. Enter through a gate into the nature reserve. Cross a small wooden bridge and ride on. Pass through 2 more gates (leaving Bewl Water onto a public lane) and climb the hill. Turn **L** into Borders Lane and enjoy the descent to The Bull pub.

Bear in mind, this will be quite a long ride by the time you've gone there and back. It avoids most, but not all, of the climbing.

2 BEDGEBURY FOREST

FOREST

GRADE: ✳✳ / ✳✳✳

DISTANCE: Family Trail – 9km (inc. 4km short loop) / 5.5 miles

Mountain Bike Trail – 13km / 8 miles

Freeride Area

MAPS: OS Explorer 136; Bedgebury Trail Map

There's so much on offer at Bedgebury that when I arrived for the first time I couldn't believe that I hadn't known about it before! I've taken my family back several times now and it has proved a hit with everybody, every time. A Sport England Grant was matched by the Forestry Commission to provide funding, and it shows.

The Family Cycle Trail does have some gradients but its hard surfaces make the forest accessible to many. There are other, easier and flatter places for families to cycle, but Bedgebury offers you the chance to cycle through the forest. Well-placed picnic tables and the bonus adventure play area will help keep small (and large) wheels turning. Even older kids can't help investigating the woodland structures.

The Singletrack Mountain Bike Trail is a tougher challenge, but it offers you the chance to experience a good variety of tracks, hone your skills on your bike and savour the peace and quiet as you spin through remote areas of Bedgebury's 2,000 acres.

It's a very good place to introduce mountain biking to new riders, young and old, as it's possible to try small sections, especially if there's no one around. Alternatively, do the whole circuit and head for some distant corners of the forest. These trails are suitable for proficient mountain bikers with good off-road skills, riding better quality off-road mountain bikes. Tracks can be remote and you may have them to yourselves, so make sure you're properly equipped with a spare tube, puncture repair kit, tools and the like. There's also a 'Freeride' area for the super brave.

kent

LINKS WITH
Traffic-free section of National Cycle Route 18, which crosses Bedgebury Forest via a good bridleway. Bewl Water (p19) is also on the other side of the A21.

CYCLE COACH
BEDGEBURY FOREST CYCLE CLUB
Offers weekly rides, a junior club, XC racing, ladies' rides and coaching. They also build trails and Bedgebury owes much to their hard work and dedication.
www.boarsonbikes.co.uk

EASY ACCESS
Although the family trail has hard surfaces, it also has significant gradients. An easier option would be the 2km Easy Access Forest Trail, which should be suitable for buggies and most wheelchairs, or even very young kids learning to ride their bikes. It heads from the Visitor Centre into the forest and circles the Play Area. Paths on the Forest Trail are smooth and wide, with a slight hill from the Visitor Centre to the Play Area. See detailed disabled access information on Bedgebury's website: *www.forestry.gov.uk/bedgebury*

PUBLIC TRANSPORT
TRAIN STATION: None nearby.

PARKING
Parking £10 (Mon–Fri), £12 (weekends and bank holidays).

BIKE HIRE
QUENCH CYCLES
The on-site hire shop has tricycles and a tramper (all terrain buggy for less able people), a bike wash, and does children's birthday parties.
T 01580 879 694
www.quenchuk.co.uk

FOOD AND DRINK
THE BEDGEBURY PINEATERY
Serves light lunches, including children's tapas. Open 10am – 5pm. Toilets.
T 07739 564 691

POINTS OF INTEREST
THE NATIONAL PINETUM
Stroll through The National Pinetum and enjoy almost 10,000 trees and shrubs. Follow a trail through one of the most amazing collections of temperate conifers in the world. Excellent children's Adventure Play Trail. Toilets at Visitor Centre.
www.forestry.gov.uk/bedgebury
www.bedgeburypinetum.org.uk

GO APE
Swing through the trees! High-rise obstacle courses where you wear a harness.
www.goape.co.uk

FAMILY RIDING
Yes! My family loved it. Younger families should be aware that there are gradients.

Follow the Forest Code
- Guard against all risks of fire.
- Protect and respect wildlife, plants and trees.
- Keep dogs under control.
- Take your litter home.
- Make no unnecessary noise.
- Take only memories away.

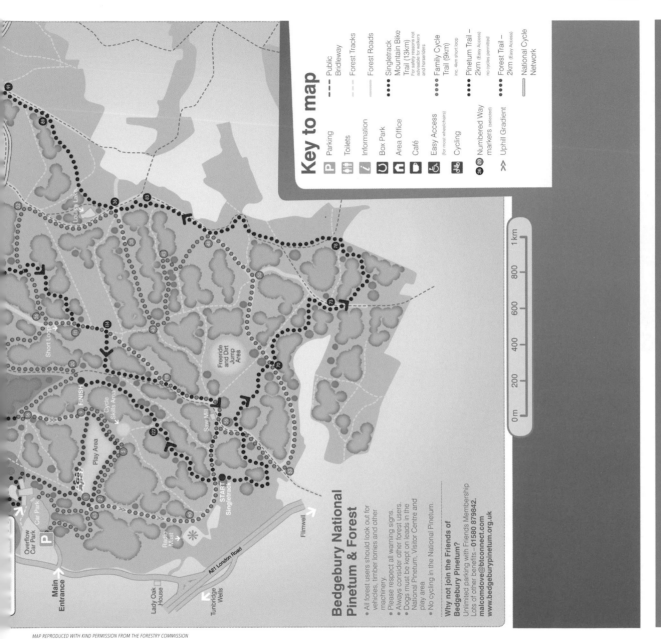

Key to map

P	Parking	--- Public Bridleway
	Toilets	---- Forest Tracks
i	Information	—— Forest Roads
↻	Box Park	•••• Singletrack Mountain Bike Trail (13km) For safety reasons not advisable for walkers and horseriders
↰	Area Office	
🏠	Café	•••• Family Cycle Trail (9km) inc. 4km short loop
♿	Easy Access (for most wheelchairs)	•••• Pinetum Trail – 2km (Easy Access) no cycles permitted
🚲	Cycling	•••• Forest Trail – 2km (Easy Access)
㊱	Numbered Way markers (selected)	—— National Cycle Network
≫	Uphill Gradient	

Bedgebury National Pinetum & Forest

- All forest users should look out for vehicles, timber lorries and other machinery.
- Please respect all warning signs.
- Always consider other forest users.
- Dogs must be kept on leads in the National Pinetum, Visitor Centre and play area.
- No cycling in the National Pinetum.

Why not join the Friends of Bedgebury Pinetum?

Unlimited parking with Friends Membership Lots of other benefits– **01580 879842.**
malcomdove@btconnect.com
www.bedgeburypinetum.org.uk

THE FAMILY CYCLE TRAIL

These paths are wide, and conglomerate or hard-surfaced. It's certainly not flat but the gradients are steady and slow rather than steep, so it should be manageable for most with baby carriages and tag-a-longs. You might get a bit of a workout though! It's worth noting that the bike shop has specially adapted cycles and a Tramper for hire. Again, expect the gradients.

There's a choice of the 4km short circuit, or the longer 9km loop. At point 56, you can ride **L** to follow the short loop joining up with the main family trail again at point 26. Alternatively, go **R** at point 56 to ride out into the depths of the forest. This longer route will take you past Louisa Lake, an excellent spot for a picnic, with a picnic table exactly where you would choose to put it.

Towards the end of the trail, there are well-spaced wooden play things with an unusual twist. If they were earlier, kids wouldn't want to get back on their bikes so the layout works well. The route finishes on a downhill, which is always a good thing.

THE SINGLETRACK MOUNTAIN BIKE TRAIL

Half the fun of the singletrack on this red-graded trail is that you never know what to expect next. The paths are varied, exciting and will keep you on your toes. There are obstacles a-plenty and it's all good fun. If you have older children who complain that flat rides are boring, let them try this. It was a hit with my family. Trails appear well maintained but this is a forest, so you do need to use your common sense and ride within your ability.

The path may be twisty and narrow and you need to look where you're going. Surfaces vary from soft, squelchy and wide, to twisty, undulating and rocky. When I went during the week, I saw other cyclists in the car park but once in the forest, I had the place to myself which is great if you want to try the trail for the first time or blast around it at speed. Make sure you don't follow the red trail after point 36 unless you know you want to do the strenuous and fairly remote loop.

The more challenging Wanda's Trail includes a small technical drop, a couple of jumps and a few berms and owes thanks to volunteers from Bedgebury Cycle Club (as do many of the trails here!). Some sections of trail are more challenging and there's a small black grade with rocky drop-offs. Drainage is good and trails should be suitable for year round riding.

The forest provides a stunning backdrop to cycle through. Light filters through the trees and there's a timeless feel to the place. You'll have so much fun that you won't notice how many little hills you're pedalling up and over until you feel it in your thighs the next day.

And as for the big hills? You'll definitely notice one or two of those...

There's also a **Freeride and Dirt Jump Area**.

3 TONBRIDGE CASTLE TO PENSHURST PLACE

with optional loop on rural bridleways & country lanes through the Weald of Kent

COUNTRY PARK   **TOURIST TRAIL**

GRADE: ✴ / ✴ ✴

DISTANCE: 8km / 5 miles (linear); 5.5km / 3.5 miles (optional loop)

MAPS: OS Explorer 147; Council / Sustrans map and guide

This is a mainly off-road route which starts in Tonbridge near the castle, park and River Medway. It runs on easy bridleways through varied landscape such as Haysden Country Park towards the Penshurst Estate in the Weald of Kent. The trail is flat except for a noticeable climb near the end. To recover, visit Penshurst House or stop for a bite to eat in the peaceful village of Penshurst.

Alternatively, those who enjoy a bit of energetic off-road riding might want to try the short optional loop through agricultural Kent.

LINKS WITH
NCR 12.

EASY ACCESS
'Squeezy' metal cycle gates are a feature of this cycle trail, thereby restricting access. However, there's a 3 mile walk at Haysden Country Park which is mainly flat along a tarmac path with hard surfaces around the lake.

DEVELOPMENT
Possible future route planned to avoid road at Lower Haysden.

PUBLIC TRANSPORT
TRAIN STATIONS: Tonbridge (30 mins from London Bridge), Leigh.

PARKING
TONBRIDGE
Tonbridge Pay and Display.
There are 2 car parks in River Lawn Road (max stay 4 hours).
Swimming Pool Car Park, the Slade, just off Tonbridge High Street, TN9 1HR. All day parking, available to non-users.

HAYSDEN COUNTRY PARK
Main car park. Follow the country park signs just to the west of Tonbridge, the park is off Lower Haysden Lane. TN11 9BE

BIKE HIRE
CYCLE-OPS
High St, Tonbridge
T 01732 500 534
www.cycle-ops.co.uk

FOOD, DRINK AND ACCOMMODATION
FORGE STORES, THE VILLAGE SHOP, PENSHURST
Closed Wed, Sat pm, and all day Sunday.

FIR TREE HOUSE TEA ROOMS, PENSHURST
Specialises in afternoon tea.
Open 2.30pm – 6pm, Wed – Sun. Also open bank holidays.
T 01892 870 382

LEICESTER ARMS HOTEL, PENSHURST
Real ales, bar snacks and a la carte menu. Comfortable and relaxing ambience. Large secluded garden. Very cyclist friendly: they helped me borrow bolt-cutters from a local garage to free my bike when I padlocked it up just moments before I realised I'd left the key at home!
T 01892 870 551
http://theleicesterarmshotel.com

POINTS OF INTEREST
HAYSDEN COUNTRY PARK
165 acres of woodland, meadow and open water, all of which provides habitat for plenty of wildlife. Play area with zip wire, public toilets with disabled access, car park at entrance.

TONBRIDGE CASTLE
Some say this is England's finest example of a motte and bailey castle, which dates back to medieval times. The 13th century gatehouse was renovated in a millennium project and now has an audio tour to help reveal the historic stories hidden within.
T 01732 770 929
www.tonbridgecastle.org

TONBRIDGE RACECOURSE SPORTSGROUND
Situated in the heart of Tonbridge, this park has crazy golf, picnic tables, a play area and loads of space for active families to let off steam. Toilets. Easy access.

PENSHURST PLACE AND GARDENS
This 'defended manor house' was once in the hands of Henry VIII who gifted it to the Sydney family. The high-ceilinged Baron's Hall is the medieval heart of the house with adjoining staterooms and the Long Gallery also worth seeing. The 11 acre formal walled gardens date back to 1346 and are a superb example of Elizabethan garden design. Toy museum, bike racks, Garden Tea Room, Venture Playground and woodland trail.
T 01892 870 307
www.penshurstplace.com

BOATS

TONBRIDGE RIVER TRIPS

Guided tours on electric river boat, and rowing boat hire, operate from below Tonbridge Castle, 50m upstream from the Big Bridge. Easter to September.
T 07808 739 020

FAMILY RIDING

Almost all off-road, this is a beautiful family ride! Squeezy gates and the large hill mean it's best suited to families where everybody's riding independently.

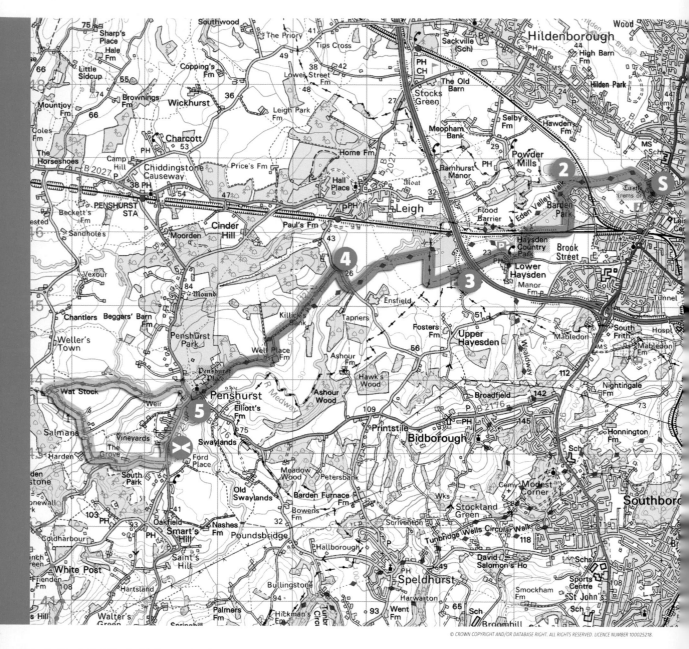

TO REACH RIVER LAWN PARKING AND START FROM TONBRIDGE STATION

With Tonbridge Station on your left, go **SA** across the roundabout. Take the first **L** into Avebury Avenue and the first **R** into River Lawn Road. There are two car parks on this road.

TO REACH THE START FROM RIVER LAWN PARKING

Ride **L** along the road. Follow the blue sign for the cycle path and swimming pool. Stay on this tarmac path. You will see a black metal sign for the swimming pool. Turn **L** towards the swimming pool, cycling across the bridge over the River Medway. Go through the gates and follow the cycle path. Ignore the entrance to the Racecourse Sportsground. Walk your bike across the bridge into the swimming pool car park.

S Swimming Pool Car Park. As if coming from the bridge, cycle through the swimming pool car park, turning to go around the model railway. Continue **SA** through the overflow car park, keeping the rugby club on your left. You should see a blue marker post for NCR 12.

Continue **SA** through the 'squeezy' metal cycle gate. Follow the track around the edge of the playing fields. Cross the bridge over the stream and ride on, following the blue NCR 12 signs. This path is flat and easy to ride. Go under the railway bridge.

2 Fork **L**, following the blue sign. There's more undergrowth and the track feels wilder. The path wends its way through the woods across a series of bridges. You should **dismount** to cross the bridges. Cross the narrow bridge over the small lake. Ride on. Turn **L** to cross another bridge... and another bridge. Take the right-hand path leading **SA**.

Ride with an open field on your right. Follow the wooden waymarker **L** signed Haysden Country Park and Penshurst. **Dismount** to cross Lucifer Bridge and then yet another bridge. At the wooden waymarker, follow the track and blue marker post into the woods and ride on.

Cross the bridge and turn **L** to follow the outer path around Barden Lake. This is easy cycling with a feeling of space; perhaps it's the views across the water? Whatever it is, it beats cycling by busy roads any day. At the end of the lake turn **L**, following the wooden waymarker to Penshurst. Ride through the brick bridge. You are now at the entrance to Haysden Country Park. Turn **L**, following the blue sign. At the end of the drive, turn **R**. Pass Acorn House on the corner. Follow the lane round to the right and ride on.

3 Just after passing beneath the concrete bridge, turn **R** into the car park but then **SA** onto a mud bridleway. Follow the blue NCR 12 sign to Penshurst. The track runs along the side of a wood where it narrows to a footpath. Here, go **R** through the squeezy gate and immediately **L** in a dog-leg to continue straight on.

The bridleway zigzags through open fields. Go through the squeezy gate into the copse. There are lots of nettles here but the path is wide enough to avoid them in most places. It's not often that you find such a well-surfaced path through woodland. Go **L**, following the wooden waymarker. Ride through the woods on this fantastic path. After the track narrows, pass a pond on your right and a WW2 pill box. Ride on.

Views open out over fields to your left. At the end of the track, pass through a squeezy gate. Turn **R** onto the road. Cross the stone bridge over the river and ride the short distance to where you can see blue signs pointing left.

4 Turn **L**, leaving the road to follow the blue signs, and cycle along the narrow, shingle path that runs between the river and the road. Turn **L** and pass through an opening in the wooden fence. You are now on Penshurst Place Estate. Ride up the concrete lane. (**NB:** *This lane is used by cars and farm vehicles.*)

Now for the only climb of the day... it's on a good, hard surface which makes it easier but it's a very definite hill and a bit of a shock to the system after all those flat bridleways!

Follow the lane left at the top of the hill, and then right passing Well Place Farm. Sweep downhill, admiring Penshurst House straight ahead of you. Watch out for the steep bend as the hill is steep.

At the base of the hill, turn **R** to visit Penshurst House and Garden. Alternatively, ride **SA** to visit the village of Penshurst (¹/₃ mile) and/or to follow our off-road optional loop. Pass through the arched stone gateway to leave the estate. Turn **R** (nasty bend on busy road) to reach Penshurst.

OPTIONAL LOOP ON AGRICULTURAL KENT BRIDLEWAYS
NB: *These are rural bridleways, sometimes muddy, uneven and with some gradients. The road link back to Penshurst is short but busy.*

5 In the middle of Penshurst village, opposite the cream tea shop, turn **R** onto the road. Pass the public toilets. Turn **L**, following the signed bridleway along the easy and pleasant path. Cross the bridge. Keep **R** at the fork, taking the dirt bridleway **SA**. This is an evil little hill, especially if you're trying to keep up with somebody a lot younger and fitter than you! Keep pedalling. At the top of the hill, enjoy the views over the Kent countryside to your right.

Reach farm buildings and turn **L** opposite a conglomerate brick and corrugated iron barn. Follow the path to join the bridleway. The track winds into trees, passing a pond on your left. It becomes rough shingle. Pass Abbotsbury Barn. Enjoy the steep descent on a smoother surface. Try not to disturb the peaceful pond, geese and oast house scene at the base of the hill. Follow the lane round as it curves.

After the brick wall, go **R** at 2 posts, turning onto the grassy bridleway. Ignore the metal gate and path on the left. Instead, follow the path round by the hedge to join the drive in front of some extremely large gates. Climb the hill and pedal round the curve to the left. Join the path **SA**. This is another fairly steep climb but at least the path is tarmac. Even if pitted, it's still easier than going uphill on mud.

Turn **L** at the road. These are busy roads: be careful. Pass the vineyard on your left. Turn **L** at the T-junction and endure a short stretch on the B2188 to return to Penshurst.

www.nationalcyclenetwork.org.uk

4 THE CRAB & WINKLE LINE

CYCLEWAY

GRADE: ✳ ✳

DISTANCE: 12km / 7.5 miles

MAPS: OS Explorer 150; Canterbury and Whitstable Tourist Information maps

The Crab and Winkle Line takes its name from the old railway line, linking ancient Canterbury with seaside Whitstable along a varied and satisfying trail. It's not dead flat, but nor are the gradients too arduous. The route runs up past the university, nips through orchards and farmland, wends its way through Clowes Wood and finally leads you into Whitstable.

We thought about doing a loop, but, when it came to it, we wanted to return via the Crab and Winkle simply because we liked it, so we reckon you'll feel the same too. There are some great views over Canterbury Cathedral, and a good stopping off point for a picnic at Winding Pond Rest Area.

We have started this route slap bang in the centre of Canterbury. I wouldn't often advocate cycling around a city, but it's a great way to soak up the atmosphere of this historic location without becoming distracted by the trappings of modern life. You may choose to stop off at Canterbury Cathedral where convenient bike racks lurk behind the walls, or why not let someone else do all the work for a change and jump in a guided rowing boat for half an hour to enjoy a waterside view of the walls? Either way, you'll cycle along some of Canterbury's characterful roads before escaping via suburban cycle paths to join the Crab & Winkle. You'll return more directly through the grounds of Canterbury University.

Whitstable is full of character. When we were there, the popular Oyster Fair was pulling in the crowds but my guess is that you'll always find fresh seafood down at the harbour. This small fishing town clearly attracts its share of tourists while retaining a certain character.

LINKS WITH

NCR 1. Want more? See Sustrans website and try the *Cathedral to Coast*, a challenging 50 mile (80km) circular ride on Regional Cycle Routes 16 and 17, linking Canterbury to Folkestone and Dover, via quiet country lanes and old villages.

EASY ACCESS

No.

DEVELOPMENT

Plans for new bridges in Whitstable – which will be part of a newly created route for pedestrians and cyclists between the existing Crab and Winkle Line at All Saints Close and the seafront – are looking like they could happen, all thanks to a coordinated approach from sustainable transport charity Sustrans and partners, Kent County Council, Canterbury City Council and The Crab & Winkle Line Trust.

PUBLIC TRANSPORT

TRAIN STATIONS: West Station, Canterbury, Whitstable.

PARKING

LONG STAY CAR PARK, ROSEMARY LANE

To reach the start: Turn **L** into Rosemary Lane and **L** again into Castle Street. Head for the cathedral. At Beer Cart Lane, turn **R** to continue on into Watling Street. At the roundabout, go **L** and pass through the bollards, following the blue cycle route sign. This is a pedestrian area with no obvious cycle path so take care and push if necessary. Pass cycle racks at the end of Rose Lane. Go across Longmarket Square and along Longmarket. Turn **L** down Burgate, through Butter Market and the main entrance to the cathedral is on your right.

BIKE HIRE AND SHOPS

KENT CYCLE HIRE, HARBOUR ROAD
T 01227 388 058
http://kentcyclehire.com

DOWNLAND CYCLES, THE MALTHOUSE OFF ST STEPHEN'S ROAD
T 01227 709 706
www.downlandcycles.co.uk

CANTERBURY CYCLE STORE, CANTERBURY
T 01227 787 880

HERBERTS CYCLES, WHITSTABLE
T 01227 272 072
www.herbertscycles.co.uk

CYCLES UK, WHITEFRIARS, CANTERBURY
T 01227 457 956
www.cyclesuk.com

FOOD, DRINK AND ACCOMMODATION
CANTERBURY

Canterbury offers a wide choice of eating options to suit most tastes and budgets.

CASTLE HOUSE, CASTLE STREET

Historic guesthouse amid the city walls. Comfortable, with helpful staff, a walled car park with CCTV. This B&B has a 'hotel' feel to it.
T 01227 761 897
www.castlehousehotel.co.uk

THE MILLERS ARMS, MILL LANE

Conveniently situated near the end of our return route into Canterbury. This is a real pub: a free house with a relaxed and comfortable atmosphere. There are railings opposite where you could lock up your bike. Accommodation too.
T 01227 456 057
www.millerscanterbury.co.uk

WHITSTABLE

Eating places are too many and varied to list specifics, but if you head for the harbour there's a good mix of stalls and other establishments. The popular Crab and Winkle Restaurant has a balcony overlooking the fishing harbour. Some interesting and idiosyncratic shops here too.

POINTS OF INTEREST

CANTERBURY CATHEDRAL

This ancient monument needs no introduction but, religious or not, the chances are that something about the interior will take your breath away. Did you know that Thomas Becket was murdered here, and that noteworthy medieval tombs include Henry IV and the Black Prince? There are bike racks inside the cathedral precinct. £12 entrance fee (£10.50 concessions). Family tickets.
www.canterbury-cathedral.org

RIVER TRIPS

WESTGATE PUNTS

Take a relaxed guided boat with this small and friendly company. Various trips available. Our route takes you past their base.
http://canterburypunts.uk

FAMILY RIDING

The off-road sections are ideal. Think about starting at the proper start of The Crab and Winkle Line. See point 3.

S Start outside the main entrance to Canterbury Cathedral. As if exiting from the cathedral and turning **R**, continue along Palace Street. Turn **L** into Alphege Street then **SA** across the road into Black Friars Street. At the old church, go **R** and **dismount** to push along this pedestrianised historic street. Ride **SA** along Black Friars Street into Mill Lane. Turn **L** into St Radigunds Street. Ride up towards Westgate Tower, one of the finest surviving medieval gateways in Britain. Following the blue NCR sign, go **R** through Towergate on the road. Turn **L** at the mini-roundabout into Westgate Grove, following another NCR sign.

2 Pass the Canterbury River Navigation Company (CRNC) boats, and stop for a river trip if you wish. You are leaving the city centre now as you follow the cycle path between the houses. Go **R**, and then **L** along Whitehall Road. Follow the blue NCR sign to Whitstable as you cycle up Whitehall Bridge Road. Head across the railway bridge and continue **SA**. Cross a road into Queen's Avenue, following the blue NCR sign.

Cycle up the road, veering **L** on the tarmac cycle path, which cuts through the grassy area. Use the pedestrian crossing and go **L** on the cycle track towards Blean. Almost immediately, turn **R** up the cycle path towards Whitstable. At the end of the track, go **SA** along Fisher Road. Turn **L** onto Westgate Court Avenue. Pedal up the hill and take a **L**. Ride round the twisting path and cycle **L** through the wooden gate to cycle around the park, following the NCR 1 sign. There's a bit of a hill on the far side. Go through the wooden gates and the track narrows, running between hedges.

Emerge onto a high track which runs along the top of a field and offers views over Canterbury, including the cathedral. Ride on towards the water tower where the path veers right. Cycle onwards, through the school grounds, passing the water tower. At the busy road, follow the pink cycle path **L**. Use the pedestrian crossing and continue on the cycle path on the opposite side of the road.

3 Turn **R** down the tarmac path, which is opposite Kent College Trade Deliveries Entrance. This is the start proper of the Crab & Winkle Line. Ride past the university buildings, passing the university car park (deserted at weekends and an ideal start point for families? No notice boards when we passed by.). Cycle **SA** on the track which passes the rugby grounds. Enjoy a smooth downhill, followed by a gravel-strewn up. Pass Blean Church on your left. There's a handy bench here too. Ride on.

Cross the road with care and follow the bridleway ahead. Ride past several fields of crops on this rural path. At the agricultural greenhouses, take the stony track to the **R** of the telegraph pole, following the NCR signs. Cross the lane and continue on the bridleway. Cycle through the woods. Follow the path **R** and enjoy this tarmac path through beautiful woodland habitat. Turn **L** at the wooden waymarker.

4 You may wish to stop at Winding Pond Rest Area. There's an unusual circular picnic table and a pond that's ripe for kids to investigate. Clowes Wood offers a habitat for a good variety of wildlife. It's part of Blean Woods Complex, one of Britain's largest areas of ancient woodland. In summer, butterflies flutter around your bike and while you may not hear the nightingales and nightjars that thrive hereabouts, you can be sure that the coo of woodpigeons will echo long after your tyre tracks have disappeared.

Continue on, enjoying this steady downhill run through pine and mixed woodland with a fair scattering of wild flowers. After the short climb, take a **L** at the fork. Enjoy this great downhill track, which leads you to a bridge across the main road. Ride on at the end of the gravel path to go through the wooden gate.

5 At the road, turn **L** towards Whitstable, following the blue sign. Join the pink cycle track and then turn **L** into Invicta Way, which forms part of the Crab and Winkle. Cycle **SA** until you reach the end of the path.

Go **L** and then **R** following the blue signs for the Crab and Winkle and the town centre. At the end of All Saint's Close, turn **R** into Seymour Avenue. At the end you'll see Whitstable Station. Ride **L** towards the harbour, then almost immediately **R** as you turn into the station forecourt, which is handy if you want to take the train back.

At the side of the station, go **L** down a track towards the Harbour. **WARNING:** *despite cycle signs there's an out-of-sight unexpected flight of stone steps here!* At the end, turn **R** and **dismount** to walk under a low bridge along Stream Walk.

Cross the road to ride along the cycleway **SA**. Cross Hamilton Road and continue along Stream Walk. Take a diagonal **L** at the blue sign, riding into Albert Street. Continue over St Peter's Road, riding on down Albert Street until you reach the High Street (Harbour Steet). Turn **R** for the Harbour.

✂ TO RETURN VIA THE UNIVERSITY

Just before point 3, where you pass the university car park, turn **L**. Cycle up Parkwood Road. At the roundabout, turn **R** onto the red cycle path. At the pedestrian crossing, cross and go over onto the red cycle track. Ride along and before you meet a road leading left, follow the cycle track **L** in through the university campus and towards Canterbury. (Easy to miss.)

Ride **L** in front of The Venue. Go **SA** across the roundabout to take the cycle path opposite. Coast along this path through a wide open green space with glimpses of Canterbury Cathedral to spur you on your way. Pass through a barrier and continue cycling **SA**.

Take a **R** and then a **L** into Lyndhurst Close, heading towards the city centre. Turn **L** into Salisbury Road. At the end of St Michael's Road, go **L** onto Beaconsfield Road. Almost immediately, turn **R** onto the cycle path and cross the park. In the corner, turn **R** and dismount for a short distance to cross Hackington Place. Head through the tunnel and then continue riding along the cycle track. Here, turn **R** for West Station or continue across the road and along the cycle path into Canterbury.

Cross at the next pedestrian crossing and continue **SA**. Ride through the housing development and emerge at a gate. Cross the road and head over the bridge over the river. Ride past the car park to join the road at St Peter's Postern, opposite St Peter's Lane near The Millers Arms and the river.

5 A SECTION OF THE VIKING COASTAL TRAIL: MARGATE TO RECULVER

with optional return to Margate via back lanes & bridleways

TOURIST TRAIL

GRADE: ✳ / ✳ ✳

DISTANCE: 13km / 8 miles (linear); 30km / 19 miles (loop)

MAPS: OS Explorer 150

This path takes you from the heart of seaside resort Margate, along the coast towards Reculver, with the sea faithfully at your side, dazzling you with its reflections. You'll ride along esplanades, beside white cliffs and through coastal meadows. On a calm day, this should be an easy and peaceful ride but by the time you reach the round tower of Reculver, you may feel more like you've been sailing rather than cycling!

Reculver is well worth a browse. Once there you have a choice: return along the Viking Coastal Trail or if you fancy something different, road happy cyclists may want to make it a circular route via the back lanes and bridleways.

Certain sections of the coastal path, for example in front of some beach huts, require you to dismount. These are clearly marked.

LINKS WITH
Viking Coastal Trail (Sandwich to Reculver) –
Sustrans Regional Route 15.
*http://explorekent.org/activities/viking-
coastal-trail/*

EASY ACCESS
The first section up to point 2 should be
accessible as there are concrete/ tarmac
surfaces with access ramps.

CYCLING FOR ALL
For information about the inclusive cycling
network across the South East, see
www.cyclinguk.org/ride/inclusive-cycling

DEVELOPMENT
None planned.

PUBLIC TRANSPORT
TRAIN STATIONS: Margate, Westgate,
Birchington-on-Sea, Herne Bay.
BUS: Reculver: Bus service No. 635 runs to the
Towers from Herne Bay, six days a week.

PARKING
MARGATE
Off The Parade, turn **L** into car park by Margate
Pier & Harbour Company (£8 per day).

Off Fort Crescent, go **R** at the brown sign for
theatres and soon **L** into Trinity Square Car Park
(£1.90).

MINNIS BAY
Car park behind the Minnis Bay restaurant,
Minnis Bay, Birchington.

RECULVER COUNTRY PARK

BIKE HIRE
VIKING COASTAL TRAIL BIKE HIRE,
MINNIS BAY CAR PARK
T 01843 843 309/07818 828 862
E vctbikes@yahoo.co.uk
www.vctbikehire.co.uk

KEN'S BIKE SHOP, MARGATE
Opposite Dreamland entrance in Eaton Road.
Collection and delivery service where possible.
T 01843 221 422
www.kensbikes.co.uk

THE BIKE SHED, MARGATE
Collection and delivery service where possible.
T 01843 228 866

FOOD ARINK
THE MINNIS BAR AND RESTAURANT
Boasts 'a passion for food.' Open all day for
food/coffee/take away. Sources meat locally
where possible. Kids' menu, outside tables.
T 01843 841 844
www.theminnis.co.uk

THE KING ETHELBERT INN, RECULVER
Pub grub, roasts and snacks. Play area
and terrace.
T 01227 374 368
www.king-ethelbert.com

CAMPING
BIRCHINGTON VALE CARAVAN PARK,
BIRCHINGTON
(on the circular loop)
T 0843 178 7070
www.parkholidays.com

ST NICHOLAS CAMPING SITE, ST NICHOLAS
AT WADE
Quiet rural site for tents and caravans,
very close to circular loop.
T 01843 847 245
www.stnicholascampingsite.co.uk

POINTS OF INTEREST
There's much more to Margate than meets
the eye. There's the Old Town, and there's
a history of smuggling in the area.

VISITOR INFORMATION CENTRE,
STONE PIER, MARGATE
T 01843 577 577
www.visitthanet.co.uk

KENT GREETERS

Margate was the first place in the world outside New York to offer this service! Meet a local volunteer who can give you inside information. Take advantage of their knowledge to discover hidden, unusual places off the tourist trail. You can even arrange to rendezvous mid cycle route with them.
www.kentgreeters.co.uk

RECULVER COUNTRY PARK

The twin towers of St Mary's Church are a distinctive feature of the coastline. The towers were added to St Mary's Church of Reculver in the 12th century. Reculver is a popular stopping-off point for migrating birds and local information is available at Kent Wildlife Trust's exhibition in the Visitor Centre. Call to find out about their latest exhibition/activities! See website for easy access details.
www.kentwildlifetrust.org.uk

FAMILY RIDING

This is an ideal family ride but perhaps not in its entirety for little ones. Head for the rock pools after Westgate (point 2) and then turn back to avoid the trickier approach to Birchington. Alternatively, start at Minnis Bay car park (point 3) and pedal to Reculver.

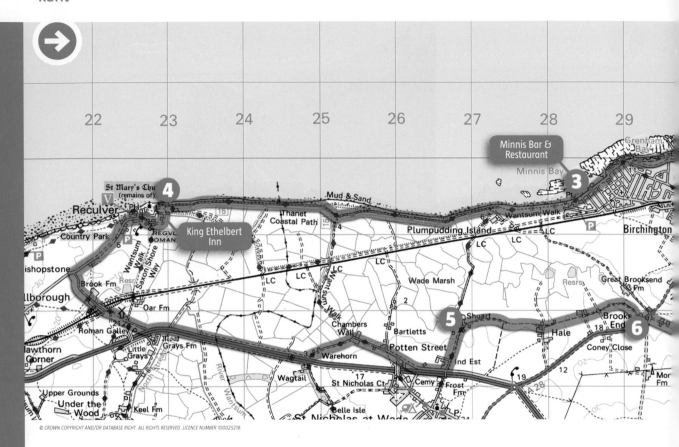

© CROWN COPYRIGHT AND/OR DATABASE RIGHT. ALL RIGHTS RESERVED. LICENCE NUMBER 100025218.

TO REACH START

Take the main road (A28) into Margate. Go **SA** at the roundabout. As it runs along the seafront, the road turns into Marine Terrace then Marine Drive then The Parade then Fort Hill then Fort Crescent (!).

S On the sea side of The Parade, opposite the Tourist Information Centre. Bike racks outside the TIC are a good place to leave your bikes if you wish to explore Margate town centre.

From the TIC, ride **L** until you see the blue cycling sign. The cycle path starts on the pavement just before the octagonal beach bar and clock tower (toilets here). You are at the heart of Margate seafront, where bright flags fly whatever the weather. Follow the Viking Coastal Trail (VCT) blue sign towards Westgate along the esplanade, keeping right of the toilets and shelter. Ride on.

Cycle **SA**, following the blue VCT sign, onto a wide concrete path above the beach. Pass Strokes Adventure golf and café. Keep an eye out on your left for the recently renovated historic

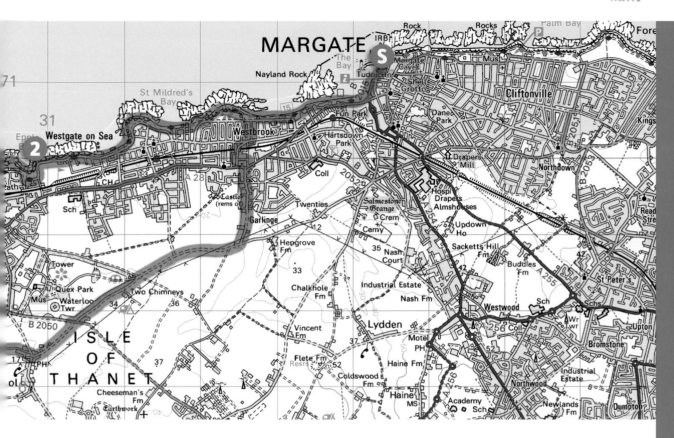

building which once operated as the prestigious Royal Spa Bathing Hospital. Pass in front of some beach huts and another café. Cycle on. Pass a large car park on your left. This is Westbrook.

The sea hereabouts is made up of a sandy shore with a chalky platform, providing marine plants and animals with plenty of rock pools and gullies where they can flourish. Keep pedalling. Cycle round, with low white cliffs on your left and the sea stretching endlessly. When you approach Westgate, **dismount**.

2 After Westgate, you have a choice:

Families with small children may wish to continue along the esplanade until a dead end is reached. Here, depending on the tide, you may go down some steps to reach various rock pools.

To continue along the VCT, go **L** following the NCR 15 trail. The cycle path is on the far side of the road. Climb the slight incline above Epple Bay. The cycle lane ends next to the golf course. Cross the road, dismount and walk down the steep path to Epple Bay, following the blue NCR 15 signs.

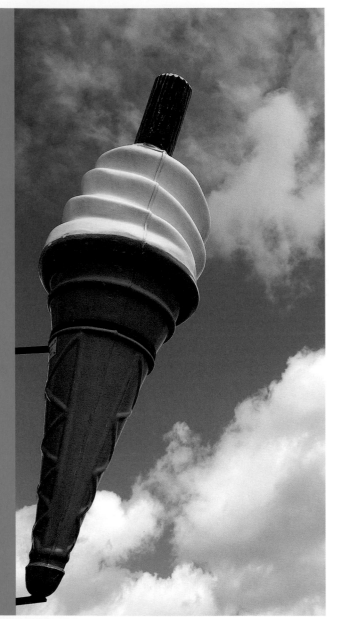

Here the concrete esplanade continues. It's narrower, but perhaps more spectacular and the cries of seagulls will speed you on your way. **Parents beware:** no safety railings and steep drop at side.

Cycle into Minnis Bay, past the beach huts. You should soon be able to see Reculver Towers in the distance. At the yellow barrier go **L**, up a slope and follow the tarmac cycle path towards the car park, passing up beside The Minnis Bar & Restaurant.

3 As you leave the car park, pass the cycle hire on your left. Cycle onwards. Go around the metal gate and ride **SA**. This section is a stunning level path which runs through meadows bordering the beach. The grasslands you're pedalling through attract a variety of butterflies including the painted lady and red admiral.

Progress should be easy here, but we were pedaling hard to move slowly into a strong headwind. We felt better when we spotted the man in front standing up to pedal as he pushed hard to keep up with his companion! The direction in which the sea breeze swirls around your pedals can make all the difference.

Ride towards the towers and you will reach them sooner or later. Pass the oyster farm on your left.

4 To explore Reculver, head **R** towards the towers and country park, café and toilets. Have a wander around. The towers are a well-known local landmark. There is also a Visitor Centre where Kent Wildlife Trust run an exhibition on renewable energy, wildlife and local information.

YOU NOW HAVE A CHOICE
You may return back along the off-road coastal path.

Or you may wish to do a circular route by following the quiet lanes and bridleways to return through the back streets of Margate onto the Viking Coastal Trail. Unfortunately this loop does include an unavoidable short section on a track alongside a dual carriageway. The only way you could avoid this would be to push your bike along a footpath leading between the coastal path and lanes.

Turn **L** in front of the towers and go along a tarmac path past the campsite, following the NCR 15 sticker on the waymarker post. Pass The King Ethelbert Inn on your left. Follow the blue Viking Coastal Trail sign as you ride along the lane. Follow Reculver Lane round as you ride in front of the café and cycle on, climbing a bit.

Turn **L** towards Chisle along Brook lane. Ride a quick up, a great down (tractors crossing!) and across the bridge over the railway. Ride **SA** at the T-junction.

Turn **L** and cycle onto the track running alongside the A299 dual carriageway. Ride on but look out for an unsignposted lane leading left. When you spot it, turn **L**. The lane curves round. Pass several houses along Potten Street.

Climb a short hill. Stay on this road, ignoring turn-offs for the A299 towards Margate. This road runs parallel with the A299 for a small distance but you won't have to get too close! Turn **L** along Stuart Lane towards Hedgend Industrial Estate.

5 At the bottom of the hill, take the bridleway leading **L**, following the green sign on the black post. The bridleway starts as concrete and then becomes stony before eventually turning to grass. It runs through fields of crops. Follow the markers to go through a gap in the hedge and the track continues, following the line of telegraph poles and the hedge up the side of the field.

Emerge at some farm buildings onto a concrete track. Ride through the farm buildings and past a beautiful farmhouse. Follow the green signs to take the bridleway opposite. This rural, easy to ride track is stunning. Cross the farm drive at the base of the slope with care and ride on and up. Go through the gate and turn **R** heading towards that busy road again.

6 Go through the gate and turn **L** onto a concrete track beside the road. There's a quick downhill run. The dual carriageway turns into a two-way road here and you need to choose a safe place to cross. Head for the lane leading **R** beside the garage, pushing your bike if you prefer. Pass Brooksend Service Station.

Turn **R**, and then almost immediately **L** into Crispe Road. Enjoy this quiet lane. At the end, turn **R**, pass The Crown & Spectre pub and almost immediately ride **L** towards Garlinge. This road can be busy as motorists use it as a shortcut. Pass Two Chimneys Camping on your right.

At the end of Margate Hill, turn **R** then almost immediately **L** into Shottendance Road. Ignore the turn-off to Westgate (Minster Road). Take the next **L** down High Street. Cycle into Garlinge, on the outskirts of Margate. At the main road, **walk** your bike across the pedestrian crossing. **Walk R**, past the shops. Ride **L** down Old Crossing Road. Soon, go **L** down Matrix Road. Ride **R**, crossing over the railway line on the bridge.

Sweep down the hill. Go **R** into Westbrook Avenue. Turn **L** into Pembroke Avenue and you can see the sea at the end. Turn **R** to rejoin the coastal pathway. Opposite Westbrook Bowls Club, look out for the opening flanked by brick gateposts behind which ramps lead to the esplanade. You are now back on the Viking Coastal Trail!

6 RIVERSIDE COUNTRY PARK

COUNTRY PARK

GRADE: *

DISTANCE: 3.2km / 2 miles (linear)

MAPS: OS Explorer 163; Country Park map

This small country park nestles in the North Kent Marshes and includes a section of Sustrans cycle path which borders the River Medway estuary. Paths are wide, well-surfaced and level. It's ideal for young or inexperienced cyclists as it offers traffic-free, easy cycling.

Of all the places that I have cycled, this is one of the most atmospheric and unusual. Shallow water is littered with abandoned yachts and discarded fishing-boats. You don't have to look far to see signs of the industrial past. As ever, wildlife and nature have adapted to make the most of any human scars on the landscape and the area includes an RSPB reserve and a Site of Special Scientific Interest.

LINKS WITH
A cycle path through Gillingham alongside the A289 which includes a short stretch along the coast. It's a built-up area with an industrial feel but if you want to cycle the extra miles, it's worth knowing that it's there. It forms a tiny part of the signed, long distance Route 1 of the National Cycle Network that connects Dover to the Shetland Islands, mainly via the east coast of England and Scotland.

EASY ACCESS
Some tracks are firm-surfaced but not all. Most are level. New play facility includes disabled swings. Access to toilets is from car park: laser key needed when centre is closed.

PUBLIC TRANSPORT
TRAIN STATIONS: Gillingham, Rainham.

TO FIND RIVERSIDE COUNTRY PARK
Driving along the B2004, you should see a brown sign. Follow the NCR 1 sign towards Copperhouse Lane.

PARKING
Small visitor centre with bike rack in car park. Car park open until 8.30pm. Public toilets. Play area.
Riverside Country Park
333 Lower Rainham Road, Rainham, Gillingham, Kent, ME7 2XH

FOOD AND DRINK
RIVERSIDE CAFÉ
Inside the visitor centre, offering snacks and hot and cold drinks.

PICNIC TABLES
Within the park.

POINTS OF INTEREST
BIRDWATCHING
Every winter, thousands of avocets, dunlins, teal and wigeons flock to the Medway – swimming in the waters, feeding on the mudflats, and flying in the skies overhead. David James, of RSPB North Kent, said: 'Watching two or three thousand dunlin flying across the water as one big cloud is absolutely spectacular. As they turn, they flash light and dark like a rippling shoal of fish. It's an amazing sight.'
Families take note: February half-term is an ideal time to take a look.

CAPSTONE FARM COUNTRY PARK
If you're looking for something off-road and more demanding, try Capstone Farm Country Park, which is also in Gillingham. This 114 hectare park has a mountain bike circuit which is proving to be popular. It's short but with some steep gradients.
www.enjoymedway.org/places-of-interest/ capstone-farm-country-park

FAMILY RIDING
Ideal for families, including the very young.

S If you come by car, and start from the visitor centre, head towards the water to find the cycle path. Maps are available inside the visitor centre. Bear **L** towards the small peninsula leading out to Horrid Hill. Despite its name, this is a stunning spot and it's well worth walking or pushing your bike the short distance along the footpath. The land stretches right into the estuary, offering sweeping 360-degree views of the water. This makes it perfect for birdwatching!

Continue away from Horrid Hill, along the cycle track. Turn **R**, following the NCR 1 sign. Leave this section of the park through a metal gate. Cycle past the car park and follow the lane through a gate. This path forms part of the Saxon Shore Way and follows the shoreline around Sharp's Green Bay and Copperhouse Marshes.

2 Eventually, after passing a large disused building on the land side, reach the edge of the country park and a small parking area. Looking out over the estuary, the industrial background of the area is made clear by the bulk of Kingsnorth Power Station beyond Nor Marsh.

To link with NCR 1, turn **L** and then **R** at the B2004. Otherwise, retrace your tyre tracks past the mishmash of abandoned boats in the mud flats. Ride past the Horrid Hill peninsula and keep cycling along the shoreline. After the private boat storage yard, go through a metal gate. Vibrant wild flowers flank the path in summer whilst the birds rule the sky. Eventually, you will reach Bloors Wharf. The wharf has various naval connections and has been used for a number of industrial purposes including ship-breaking. The path veers slightly away from the water to reach a wooden waymarker.

3 You are at Motney Hill. Turn **R** onto Motney Hill and then **L** into Rainham Dock East, another small section of the park. Follow the track and the NCR 1 as it leads you towards the B2004.

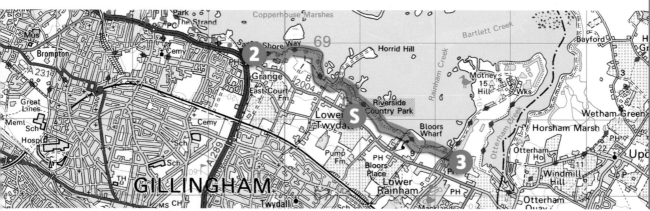

east sussex

east sussex

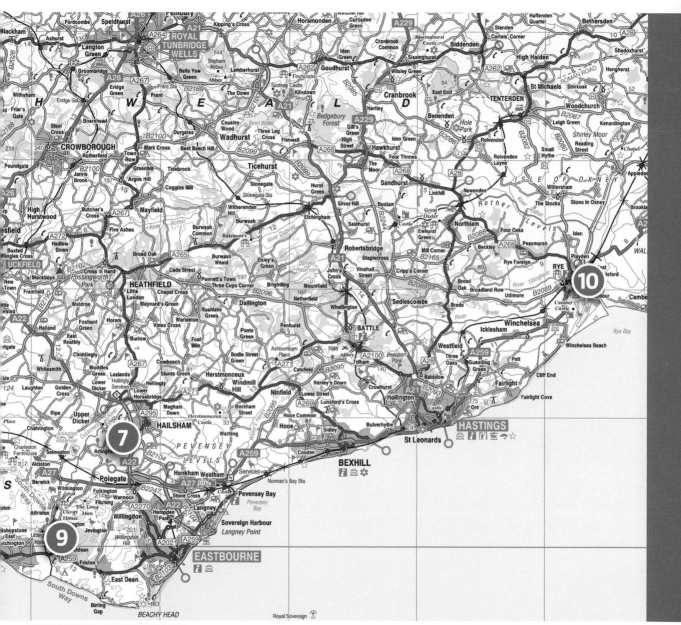

CONTAINS ORDNANCE SURVEY DATA © CROWN COPYRIGHT AND DATABASE RIGHT

7.1 CUCKOO TRAIL
& extension to Eastbourne

CYCLEWAY	TOURIST TRAIL
GRADE: ✳ / ✳ ✳	
DISTANCE: 22km / 13.5 miles	
MAPS: OS Explorer 123. Or pick up the Cuckoo Trail guide	

The Cuckoo Trail runs from Heathfield to Polegate along the path of the old Cuckoo Line railway. It was called the Cuckoo Line after the tradition that the first cuckoo of spring was heard at Heathfield Fair.

The outstanding feature of the Cuckoo Trail is the sheer length of this hard-surfaced, off-road trail, especially now that the trail has been extended to reach Hampden Park Station in Eastbourne. Families might prefer to start at Polegate if they want a nice, easy level section. If you want more of a workout, the stretch between Hailsham and Heathfield offers the chance for a gradual, steady climb. You'd be well advised to cycle north first, to ensure a nice easy run back home. Or, for those who like to take it easy, how about planning a leisurely ride to the craft barn?

For cyclists who enjoy off-road riding and the chance to explore, we include optional loops to Abbot's Wood and Michelham Priory. We've also found some handy pit stops, relaxing cafes and even a couple of campsites. Why not make a weekend of it? You could leave your car doors firmly locked and explore by bike!

east sussex

LINKS WITH
NCR 21.

EASY ACCESS
Generally hard-surfaced, mainly tarmac, wide paths. Watch out for the steady uphill gradient as you travel north from Hailsham to Heathfield.

CYCLING FOR ALL
For more information about the inclusive cycling network across the South East, see *www.cyclinguk.org/ride/inclusive-cycling*

PUBLIC TRANSPORT
TRAIN STATIONS: Hampden Park, Eastbourne, Polegate.

PARKING
SHINEWATER PARK
Easy roadside near Shinewater Park.

POLEGATE
Easy roadside on Levett Road.

OLD LOOM MILL CRAFT CENTRE
Car park at Old Loom Mill Craft Centre, if you're using the cafe or buying crafts.

HAILSHAM
Free car park off South Road in Hailsham is directly on the Cuckoo Trail.

BIKE HIRE
CYCLE REVIVAL, HAILSHAM ROAD, HEATHFIELD
T 01435 866 118
www.cyclerevival.co.uk

MP CYCLE HIRE, HAILSHAM
T 01323 449 245

CUCKMERE CYCLE COMPANY
At the Seven Sisters Country Park, a short drive away.
T 01323 870 310
www.cuckmere-cycle.co.uk

FOOD AND DRINK
ON ABBOT'S WOOD/MICHELHAM LOOP
YEW TREE INN, ARLINGTON VILLAGE
Classic country pub, Harveys ale, large garden with climbing frame, wide menu with large portions, children's menu.
T 01323 870 590
www.yewtree-inn.co.uk

ARLINGTON TEA GARDENS
Open Wed – Sun 10am – 5pm, Fri 11am – 5pm
T 01323 484 549

OLD OAK INN, ARLINGTON
Open all day at weekends. Climbing frame for kids.
T 01323 482 072

DIRECTLY ON THE CUCKOO TRAIL
OLD LOOM MILL CRAFT CENTRE
AND TEA ROOM
BN26 6QX. Open 9am – 5pm every day except Christmas and New Year. Pleasant tearoom that serves simple hot and cold meals and cakes. There's an outside terrace with views to the Downs and – all-important for parents – somewhere for kids to play. Toilets. Eclectic mix of stalls to browse.

Picnic tables here and there, notably at Hailsham Common Pond.

THE CUCKOO SHACK CAFE
Priory Court Farm, Sayerlands Lane, Polegate BN26 6QX.
See Facebook page for pre-booking for cycling groups and opening hours.
www.priorycourtfarm.co.uk/ Priory_Court_Farm/Cuckoo_Shack.html

WITHIN THROWING DISTANCE
CUCKOO REST, HELLINGLY
T 01323 440 745
www.cuckoorest.co.uk

WESSONS CAFE, HORAM
Open Wed – Sun. Listed as one of the top five bikers' cafés in Observer Food Monthly magazine. Proximity to Cuckoo Trail also makes this cafe popular with cyclists and walkers.
T 01435 813 999
www.wessonscafe.com

THE HORAM INN
Welcomes cyclists and can provide secure overnight cycle parking. Just off NCR 21.
T 01435 812 692
www.horaminn.co.uk

HORAM MANOR FARM
Lakeside Cafe & Bar
T 01435 408 015
www.lakesidecafehoram.co.uk

RUNT IN TUN PUB AND CAMPSITE
Comfortable, cyclist-friendly, pub snacks and specials, use local suppliers where possible. Campsite to rear of pub.
T 01435 864 284
www.runtintun.co.uk

POLEGATE, HAILSHAM AND HEATHFIELD
All have a small cross-section of eating places.

ACCOMMODATION
PEEL HOUSE FARM CARAVAN PARK, POLEGATE
This is low-key camping at its best! A small, peaceful site in open farmland with views of the Downs, a small play area and friendly owners. ⅔ of a mile up the lane from the Cuckoo Trail, also via gate at the adjacent Old Loom Centre and via a footpath.
Min 20ft distance between tents, overflow field in peak times, four statics for hire.
T 01323 845 629
www.peelhousefarm.com

HORAM MANOR TOURING PARK HORAM, NEAR HEATHFIELD
Medium size campsite set in woodland amidst Area of Outstanding Natural Beauty. Horse riding, fishing and craft sessions on estate. See website for easy access info.
T 01435 813 662
www.horam-manor.co.uk

THE HORAM INN
Welcomes cyclists and can provide secure overnight cycle parking. Just off NCR 21.
T 01435 812 692
www.horaminn.co.uk

POINTS OF INTEREST
ABBOT'S WOOD
Coppicing hazel and hornbeam for firewood has helped make this Forestry Commission woodland an important site for butterfly and dormouse conservation. Informal cycling is permitted on forest roads but please respect the environment. The wood is named Abbot's Wood because, during the reign of Henry I, it was gifted to Battle Abbey and overseen by the Abbot (hence Abbot's Wood).

MICHELHAM PRIORY
This tucked away, yet interesting, historic building is owned by Sussex Past. Entry to the Priory is just after the bike racks by the gatehouse. Cross a stone bridge over the medieval moat and walk through an imposing 14th Century Gatehouse. Michelham Priory dates from 1229. Replica Iron Age village reached from Moat Walk. Guided tours. Extensive gardens. Nature Trail. Restaurant. Gift shop. Mill.

FAMILY RIDING
The Cuckoo Trail is great for family riding. Any links that are road sections are short, with pavements where youngsters could push if need be.

OPTIONAL LOOPS
Families with young children should note that you can reach the tearoom at Arlington with virtually no road cycling. Michelham and the pub/reservoir are for road-happy cyclists only.

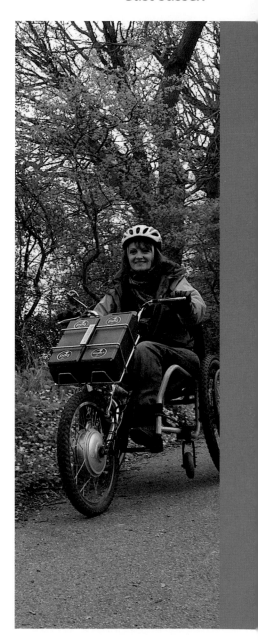

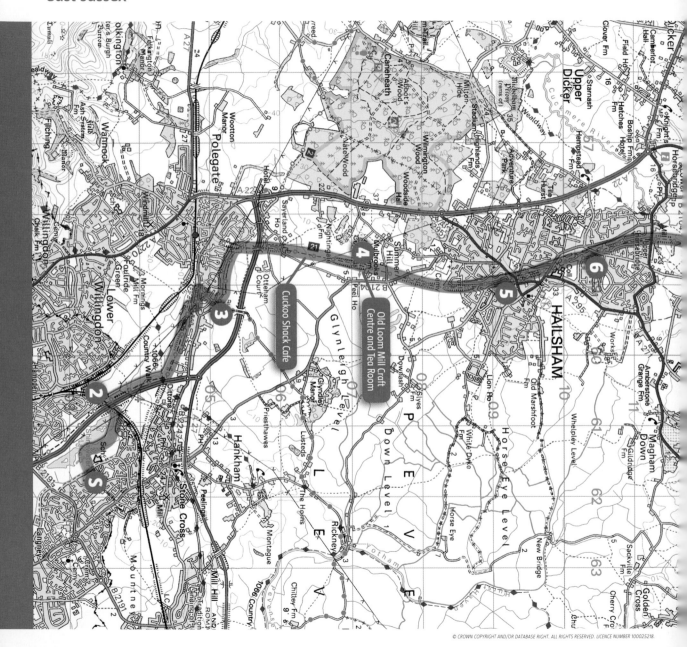

Cuckoo Shack Cafe

Old Loom Mill Craft Centre and Tea Room

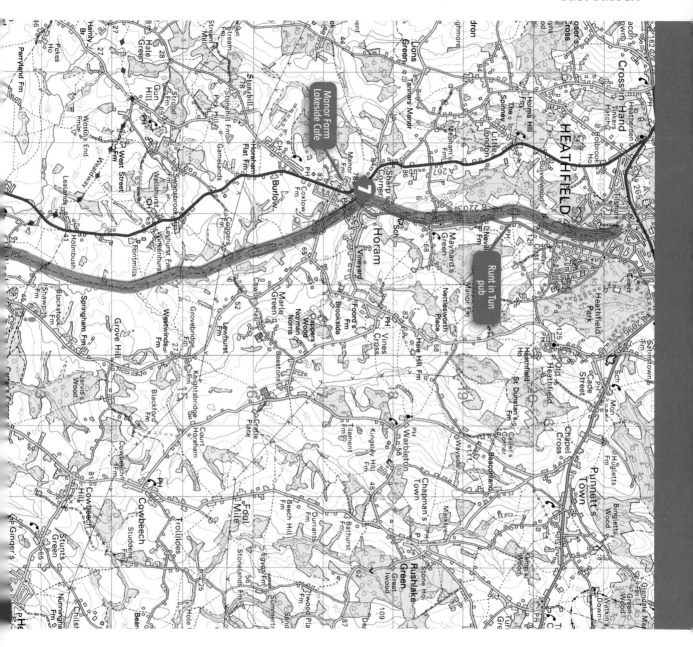

Manor Farm
Lakeside Cafe

Runt in Tun
pub

SHINEWATER PARK, EASTBOURNE TO POLEGATE (5km/3 miles)
We've started the extension from Shinewater Park, Eastbourne.
This is a small park with a play area and a couple of small fishing
lakes. It has limited facilities but provides a good base to set out
from. There's plenty of roadside parking hereabouts.

TO REACH SHINEWATER
Driving from Polegate on the A27, turn **R** at the roundabout onto
the A22. Go **SA** at the next roundabout, staying on the A22 and
look out for the lakes on your left. Go **L** at the next roundabout
just after the lakes. Turn **L** after The Mill pub into Larkspur Drive
and you'll soon see the park entrance on your left.

S There are several ways that you could join the Cuckoo Trail
extension to Polegate. I suggest that from the entrance on
Fletching Road, you head off **R** on the gravel cycle path. The park's
level paths are ideal for little kids who are learning to ride. Join the
tarmac cycleway that stretches the length of the park.

2 Zip through the tunnel under the A22 and you will see a sign
R for the Cuckoo Trail/ NCR 21. It's 2.5 miles to the Cuckoo
Trail from here. Cross the humpback bridge over the water and
ride on. At the fork, go **R** following the Cuckoo Trail sign up the
slope. For a short stretch, the Cuckoo Trail runs alongside the A22
but don't be put off: once over the bridge, the path runs at the
bottom of an embankment.

As you climb the next hill, views towards Willingdon and the
South Downs open up. This stretch along the A22 is fairly new and
does the handy job of linking the Cuckoo Trail with town and coast.

Turn **R**, following the Cuckoo Trail sign. Ride on the compacted
gravel path. Follow the NCR blue signs to link you with the next
stretch of the Cuckoo Trail.

Go **L**, then **R** into Aberdale Road, then **L** onto the cycle path
running alongside the busy Pevensey Road. Cross at the pedestrian
crossing and continue on the cycle path to your left. Turn **R** along
Levett Road.

3 **POLEGATE TO HAILSHAM** (4km/2.5 miles)
*(SAT NAV Junction of Levett Rd and Shepham Lane. Polegate
BN26.)* This is one of the access points to the Cuckoo Trail in
Polegate. Others may be found at School Lane, Otham Court Lane
and Sayerland Lane.

From this access point, ride this tarmac path beneath the trees.
*(At the fork, turn **L** to leave the trail for the centre of Polegate.)* Cycle
R for Hailsham. Pass a picnic table on your left and then cross the
bridge over the non-stop A27 and cycle **SA**.

OPTIONAL LOOP
This is where the Optional Loop to Abbot's Wood separates
from the Cuckoo Trail. Turn **L** if coming from Eastbourne, **R** if coming
from Hailsham. See loop directions on p73.

Continue **SA**. Along the Cuckoo Trail, look out for various sculptures
and features relating to local points of interest, safe road crossings,
access points and seating, all designed as part of a project aiming
to draw our attention to the 'travelling landscape'. Pass the lane
on your right that leads to the campsite.

4 Look out for the gate on your right which leads to the Old Loom Mill Craft Centre and Tea Room – ideal if you fancy a quick stop. Otherwise, ride on.

The tarmac path reaches a gate with several small sculptures as you reach Freshfield Close. You are now in Hailsham. Cyclists must **dismount** for this short stretch of footpath. Ride **SA** down Freshfield Close. Turn **R** into Lindfield Drive, following the brown Cuckoo Trail sign. Turn **L**, still following the brown signs, along Station Road.

Pass Hailsham Common Pond with picnic tables and bike racks on your right. Be careful here: this is a busy stretch of road but children could push along the pavement. At the top of the road, you are in Hailsham town centre. (*Follow the main road round to the right to find various eating places.*)

Turn **L** into the car park, following the brown Cuckoo Trail sign.

5 **HAILSHAM TO HORAM** (9km/5.5 miles)
Turn **R** through the underpass. Cycle along the tarmac path through a brick tunnel. Ride up the slope and continue **SA**, forking **L** through the metal arch. The school playing fields should be on your right. At the road, cyclists must follow the road **R**, leaving the footpath to the pedestrians. Turn **L** back onto the cycleway at the base of the road. Pass under a couple of bridges and come to a T-junction of tarmac paths.

6 To stay on the Cuckoo Trail, ride to your **R** following the wooden Cuckoo Trail sign. (*This is the junction which our optional Abbot's Wood loop returns to.*)

The trail runs between houses along the top of a small embankment. Cross the Upper Horsebridge Road at the pedestrian crossing and ride on. Countryside views open up along this stretch of rural path. Pass Hellingly Station, now a private dwelling, and Hellingly Millenium Arboretum.

Signs warn of a steep descent, probably because there's a road at the base. The road leads into Hellingly. Continue straight back up the small slope to cycle onwards. Cross the bridge over the River Cuckmere. Follow the NCR 21 and Cuckoo Trail signs **SA**. Not surprisingly, as it leads you through the Sussex countryside, you may find that this path is well used by dog walkers and horse riders. Notice the intricate metal sculpture on Cattle Creep Bridge.

Pedal up a gradual but long climb. At the top, cycle through the tunnel. To your right, notice the first exit for Horam. The next exit is better for the town centre and camping. Ride onwards. At Downline Close, cross the road, with care, and ride **SA** on a tiny stretch of brick path. (*To head into Horam or use the public toilet (portaloo!), ride **L** and then **R** into Hillside Drive.*)

7 **HORAM TO HEATHFIELD** (4km/2.5 miles)
Otherwise, to continue on the Cuckoo Trail to Heathfield, follow the blue NCR 21 sign **SA** along the tarmac path. (*For Merrydown Cider and the Hidden Spring Vineyard, follow the sign up the hill on the **R** fork.*) For the Cuckoo Trail, ride **SA** on the **L** fork.

Climb another hill, go across Hendalls Farm Bridge and keep pedalling. On the approach to the road crossing, follow the NCR 21 sign up and across the bridge. Climb another long, steady gradient. When you cross Maynards Green Bridge, you're almost at the top! (Notice the wooden waymarked footpath on your right? This leads a short distance to the Runt in Tun Pub: a nice handy place to stop!) Alternatively, near the top of the hill, there's a handy bench and picnic table. The sign says a mile to Heathfield but in fact you're almost at the outskirts.

At the end of the tarmac path, cross the busy road to go **R**, following the brown Cuckoo Trail and NCR 21 signs. Go down the slope between the metal railings, cross Ghyll Road and continue on into Heathfield. It's around this time that it dawns on you that you have, in fact, been climbing one big hill as this stretch of the Cuckoo Trail is all up. Still, it's a gentle hill: not too painful. See the metal cuckoo sculpture as you reach the end of the trail, and the chance to explore Heathfield, safe in the knowledge that the way back will be all downhill.

7.2 CUCKOO TRAIL
& optional loop to Abbot's Wood & Michelham Priory

CYCLEWAY	TOURIST TRAIL
GRADE: ✴ ✴ / ✴ ✴ ✴	
DISTANCE: 13km / 8 miles	
MAPS: OS Explorer 123	

This loop is good if you like some variety in your cycling. It covers a mix of hard-surfaced cycleways and bridleways, off-road bridleways through woodland and farmland, and some cycling on mainly quiet lanes, which could lead you to a classic country pub, a tea room or Michelham Priory. The choice is yours. Energetic families should enjoy the bridleways in Abbot's Wood. If you wish to avoid crossing the busy dual carriageway and any road cycling, think about returning via Abbot's Wood too. As ever, off-road bridleways may be muddy in wet conditions.

LINKS WITH
NCR 21.

PARKING

OLD LOOM MILL CRAFT CENTRE

Car park at Old Loom Mill Craft Centre if you're using the café or buying crafts.

ABBOT'S WOOD CAR PARK

Pay and display, toilets, adventure play area, barbecues (first come, first served basis, bookable for groups) and a picnic site leading to forest walks. There is also a large grass area for ball games.
www.forestry.gov.uk

TO REACH THE START

The Old Loom Mill Craft Centre is not in the most accessible place yet it provides a great start/finish point for families because of its facilities. In Polegate, turn **L** at the A27/Polegate Bypass. Drive for ½ mile then, at the roundabout, take the 2nd exit onto the A22. Soon, turn **L** towards Bay Tree Lane. Follow the lane to a T-junction where you turn **R** into Bay Tree Lane. Follow the lane round: it becomes Sayerland Lane. At the B2104, turn **L**. The Craft Centre is next door to the Caravan Park on your left.

The Craft Centre is happy for people to use their car park if they use the cafe and/or browse the stalls.

S Exit from the car park through the gate behind the main building. This leads directly onto the Cuckoo Trail and is open the same hours as the Craft Centre. Turn **L** onto the Cuckoo Trail.

2 As you approach the large bridge over the busy A22, look out for the signs towards Abbot's Wood and NCR 2. Turn **R** along the bridleway, leaving the Cuckoo Trail.

Ride parallel to this busy road for a short distance. Stay on the bridleway at Sayerland Lane, following the track round to take the bridleway heading **L**, in the direction of the NCR 2 sign.

Go through the tunnel, passing under the A22. Cycle with Cophall Farm and Premier Inn on your left and continue on the public bridleway, following the NCR 2 sign. You are heading away from the Cuckoo Trail. By the steps, turn **L**, passing through the gate and still following the NCR 2 sign.

Where you meet another track, turn **L** in order to go straight on. Look out for the NCR 2 signs on the canisters. Ride up the steady incline, admiring the views of the Downs to your left. Stay on this track, following the NCR 2 signs, and enjoy the downhill run.

3 At the crossroads, go **SA** following the signs for Abbot's Wood Cycle Ride.

OPTIONAL LOOP

During wet weather, this bridleway can become very churned up due to heavy use. If need be, turn **R** along Robin Post Lane. This path is initially level, gradually climbing through beautiful woodland. Look for a graveled forest road (4th path on **L**, metal gate) heading west off Robin Post Lane. Stay on this zigzagging gravel path, ignoring offshoots. It is unsigned. Ride **L** up this wide shingle and mud path. At the end, reach a junction and go **L**, staying on the shingle path. Turn **R** at the next junction, riding on the shingle track. Ride downhill and, at the junction, go **L** following the track round and ignoring grassy turn-offs. At the crossroads, either follow the Forest Road **R** to emerge opposite the Old Oak Inn or continue **SA** to rejoin the Abbot's Wood Cycle Ride bridleway.

Reach a path with a green bridleway sign. Turn **R** and cycle towards the road.

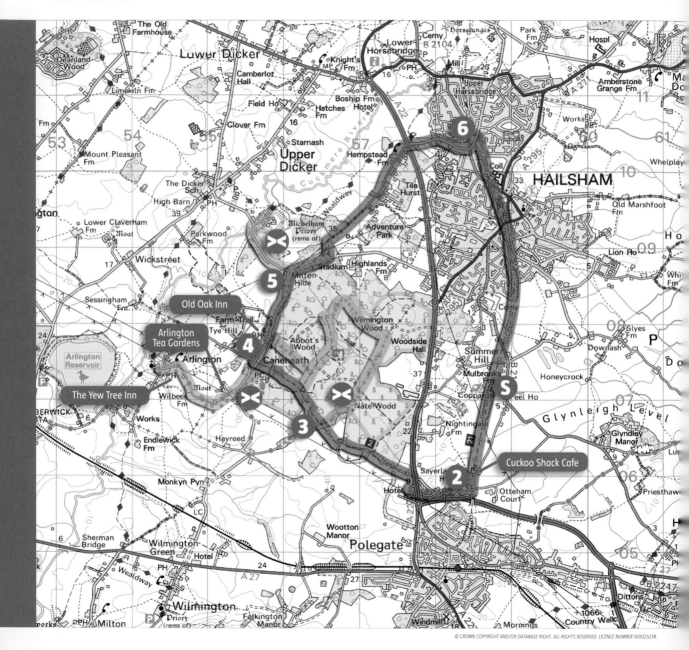

Old Oak Inn

Arlington
Tea Gardens

The Yew Tree Inn

Cuckoo Shack Cafe

4 Emerge at the lane.

OPTIONAL LOOP
Turn **L** for the tea room and the pub at Arlington. Pass a road (Tye Hill) on your right. Pass Abbott's Wood Car Park (toilets) on your left. Ignore Bayleys Lane on your left. Ride on along Wilbees Road. Pass Arlington Tea Gardens and then Wilbees Farm. Wilbees Road turns into The Street. Keep riding and you will find the Yew Tree Inn tucked away on a corner in the small village of Arlington. Linger at the pub if you wish, then turn **L** to retrace your tyre tracks and to continue on our circuit.

Turn **R** for Michelham and to return to the Cuckoo Trail on roads. In one or two places this route can be busy and is not ideal for young children. Ride up a slight slope, pass the Old Oak Inn on your left. Sweep downhill.

5 At the triangular junction, watch out: it's a busy road!

OPTIONAL LOOP
Go **L** for Michelham Priory. Cycle along Arlington Road West towards Upper Dicker. Cross a narrow bridge shortly before you see the entrance to Michelham Priory on your right. Don't miss the water mill (flour for sale) as you enter the car park.

Go **R** along Arlington Road West to return to the Cuckoo Trail. Find the bridleway. Ignore the first bridleway at the low white fence with the waymarker sign. Ride on and look for a layby with concrete blocks and a blue sign to the Cuckoo Trail. Head forwards on the main track. There's a bit of a climb but don't worry, you'll soon be heading downhill. Enjoy the off-road downhill through the woods, sticking to the main track. Sections may be a little bumpy! Emerge at gateposts. Ride **SA** onto a tarmac lane.

At the end of the road, follow the marked cycle path on your **R** to cross the dual carriageway. It's a very fast and busy road. Ride **SA**, cycling up Hempstead Lane and following the blue sign for the Cuckoo Trail. At the first roundabout, take the 2nd exit, going **SA**. At the second roundabout, take the second exit **L** signed down Hawks Road towards the Cuckoo Trail. Where the road rises, opposite the crash barrier, turn **L**, following the Cuckoo Trail sign.

6 At the wooden Cuckoo Trail sign, turn **R** for Hailsham. Ride on following the Cuckoo Trail bike signs. At the estate road, turn **R** and then **L** back onto the Cuckoo Trail. Go past the school and, after the metal arch, fork **R** to cycle down the slope. Ride on, staying on the Cuckoo Trail. Pass through a tunnel and emerge at a car park. Turn **L** and then **R** onto Station Road. This is a short stretch of busy road with lots of parked cars but there is pavement alongside to push if necessary.

Opposite Hailsham Common Pond (picnic tables), turn **R** into Lindfield Drive and **L** into Freshfield Close, following the Cuckoo Trail signs. Dismount for a short, narrow stretch of footpath. Enjoy this wide, easy stretch of the Cuckoo Trail looking out for the Old Loom Mill Craft Centre on your left.

8 DEERS LEAP PARK

COUNTRY PARK

GRADE: ✳ ✳ / ✳ ✳ ✳

DISTANCE: 240 acres with a variety of short trails (family / singletrack / some north shore) to choose from. Family trail is roughly 4 miles, depending on choice of path.

MAPS: Deers Leap Park provide a trail map free of charge; OS Explorer 135.

Deers Leap Park is an ideal place to see what you and your mountain bike can do off-road. My kids were bowled over by it. They loved the fact that they could try a variety of trails and features without having to ride for miles in between them! Any gradients are easily manageable.

LINKS INDIRECTLY WITH
Sustrans NCR 21 along Worth Way (Crawley – East Grinstead). Also Forest Way (Groombridge – East Grinstead). See *Cycling in Sussex*.

EASY ACCESS
No.

DEVELOPMENT
Ongoing plans include technical rides and features for more experienced riders, such as a wider variety of north shore.

PUBLIC TRANSPORT
TRAIN STATION: **East Grinstead (not nearby).**

PARKING
On site.

FURTHER INFORMATION AND BIKE HIRE
DEERS LEAP BIKES, EAST GRINSTEAD
Bike hire, test centre, repairs, servicing.
T 01342 325 858
http://deersleap.co.uk

FOOD AND DRINK
Café on site.

POINTS OF INTEREST
TREKCO
A range of outdoor activities for individuals, families, schools and corporate groups. This includes Mountain Bike Extreme birthday parties at Deers Leap Park, which may be done in conjunction with other activities such as High Ropes, Tunnels, Archery, Abseiling or Rock Scramble.
www.trekco.com

FAMILY RIDING
Loads of potential at this location for introducing kids to mountain biking and developing their skills.

Set in 240 acres on a working farm, there's a relaxed, friendly feel to Deers Leap. On arrival, call in at the shop and pay a small fee per person (£2.50 at time of writing).

There's an all-weather bike track and, as you follow it, you can veer off into any of the woodland areas to discover singletrack with a mix of extra features: jumps, bumps, dips, curves, roots, stones and plenty of mud too. There's a real mix of stuff to suit all abilities and ages. The park was taken over by TrekCo, an outdoor education company, in 2009 and, whenever possible, the owners add in new features to the woodland trails.

I gave my kids the map and they loved choosing which way to go. You won't get lost because there are plenty of numbered marker posts and Deers Leap is a manageable size. The park offers the opportunity to mountain bike without riding in an isolated area. You know there's help reasonably nearby should you need it and the map has an Accident Emergency Procedure on the back.

As you ride, the views are more than worthy of an Area of Outstanding Natural Beauty. There are picnic tables here and there, or you can head back to the reasonably-priced cafe for hot drinks and chocolate. Not a bad thing in our climate: we'd just settled down to a picnic when the heavens opened and a hot drink was a welcome alternative.

There's a tricky stretch of north shore in Cock Robin Wood which, to my eye, looked horribly high (4 or 5 foot off the ground) but I'm told you're not meant to fall off! I'm afraid I didn't test it out but I was happy to try the low stretch in the Duck Paddock. We all enjoyed riding across the wooden bridges, some of which are quite long but reasonably wide while others are shorter but narrower.

If you're there as a group of mixed riders, and some of you don't like singletrack, the way the park's laid out means that some riders can stick to the all-weather track and others can be more adventurous. Providing you know your kids will ride within their ability, and there are some advanced features here, it's also the sort of place you'd be happy to give them a bit of freedom to explore.

We finished our day by visiting the bike wash. This was surprisingly popular with my kids who not only washed their own bikes but mine too. Can't be bad!

It's worth mentioning that my son decided to hold his birthday party here and he told me on our way home that it was the best birthday party he's ever had. They all enjoyed listening to the instructor's tips and advice and each of the children came away feeling pleased with themselves. It's a great option for kids who like bikes and are happy riding off-road.

9.1 SEVEN SISTERS COUNTRY PARK

FOREST	COUNTRY PARK

GRADE: ✳

DISTANCE: 1.6km / 1 mile

MAPS: OS Explorer 123; download a PDF of the easy access trail at Seven Sisters from: *http://tinyurl/7SistersEasyAccess*

Responsible cyclists are welcome at Seven Sisters Country Park. While there are no bridleways in the Park, cycling is permitted on the valley floor. There is a concrete track which offers safe access to the beach: easy cycling and ideal for young families and easy access. It can be busy at weekends.

The track runs alongside the River Cuckmere and offers views of the spectacular Cuckmere meanders and Seaford Head. Where the concrete track finishes, cyclists may wish to padlock their bikes up and continue along the path of loose stones to the shingle beach. The white cliffs provide a stunning backdrop to the English Channel and it's a gorgeous, if sometimes windswept, spot for a picnic. Just be sure to keep your rubbish and wrappers out of the wind's way so that you can take them safely home with you!

The South Downs Way runs through the Park but this section is a footpath only, so cycling is not permitted on this route. Bike racks can be found next to the Shepherd's Caravan near the Visitor Centre.

LINKS WITH
NCR 2.

EASY ACCESS
Not in the forest, but the concrete path which runs through Seven Sisters Country Park to Foxhole should be accessible to most. Full details of the 2km easy access trail, including a downloadable, detailed map, can be found at: *www.sevensisters.org.uk*

DEVELOPMENT
Locals, including the Cycle Seahaven group, are campaigning for an official singletrack trail which would run from the top of the forest near the Gallops area, as well as adoption of the very popular, but unofficial, downhill route. See *www.cycleseahaven.org.uk* for club information, including organised rides in Friston Forest.

PUBLIC TRANSPORT
TRAIN STATION: Seaford Station is on NCR 2.

HOW TO GET THERE
The entrance to Seven Sisters Country Park is on the A259 at Exceat between Newhaven and Eastbourne.

PARKING
Friston Forest is behind Seven Sisters Country Park. By Exceat Bridge, leave the A259 to turn towards Litlington. Turn **R** into the first car park marked Seven Sisters Country Park. This offers direct access to the marked forest trails, visitor centre, café, toilets and other facilities. Also, directly off the A259, there's a car park with an ice cream van. Park here and you're

on the right side of that busy road for the easy access trail in Seven Sisters Country Park. The Butchershole car park (no facilities) for the Jeremy Cole MTB Trail, is approx 1km north of Friston on the Friston-Polegate road.

BIKE HIRE AND SHOPS
SEVEN SISTERS CYCLES
Reached via top of the car park behind the Visitor Centre. Trail maps for Friston Forest Family and Jeremy Cole MTB Trail are available here. Bike hire: mountain bikes with front suspension, hybrid/comfort bikes, tandems, children's bikes, children's buggies, child seats, and helmets included for all children. Pre-booking advised. Temporarily closed: check website.
T 01323 870 310
www.cuckmere-cycle.co.uk

MR.CYCLES
Bike sales, repairs, clothing and accessories. See *Where to Ride* page on website for more Friston Forest routes and loops.
T 01323 893 130
www.mrcycles.co.uk

FOOD, DRINK AND ACCOMODATION
EXCEAT FARMHOUSE
Traditional café offering teas and light lunches. Two en suite rooms. Shed where bikes can be locked away for B&B guests.
T 01323 870 218

THE GUESTHOUSE EAST, EASTBOURNE
Secure cycle storage and possibly bikes available to borrow at this cross between a B&B and self-catering establishment.
T 01323 722 774
www.theguesthouseeast.co.uk

LITLINGTON TEA GARDENS
Traditional teas in a spacious genteel garden setting. Some tables under cover.
T 01323 870 222

POINTS OF INTEREST
SEVEN SISTERS COUNTRY PARK
Is situated in an Area of Outstanding Natural Beauty. The Park has a Visitor Centre with exhibition area and shop with local crafts, plus toilets. The Parkland includes white cliffs, chalk downlands and a shingle beach. The River Cuckmere meanders along the valley floor attracting a wide variety of wildlife and, also, the odd canoeist!
In fact the chalk downland and geological interest of the park have caused it to be graded as a Site of Special Scientific Interest. The Park offers wildlife a diverse mix of habitats such as grassland, woodland, wetland, and coastal and marine. For detailed information on the birds you may be privileged enough to see here, go to the *birdwatching* section on *www.sevensisters.org.uk*

FAMILY RIDING
Young families should enjoy the concrete track along the valley floor in Seven Sisters, or the flatter section of the forest family trail. For older families, the forest is a great environment to explore, not only *with* your bike but *what* your bike can do.

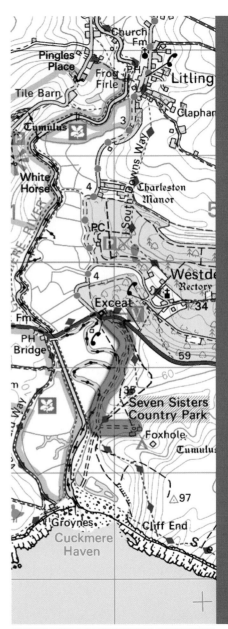

9.2 FRISTON FOREST FAMILY CYCLE TRAIL

FOREST   COUNTRY PARK

GRADE: ✱ ✱

DISTANCE: 7km / 4.5 miles

MAPS: OS Explorer 123

Friston Forest is a substantial forest and hidden away beneath its canopy is a surprising number of tracks. Its undulating terrain makes it a popular place for walkers and mountain bikers and its quieter valleys offer a haven for wildlife such as occasional deer or rare butterflies like the fritillaries.

If you like to know where you're going and what to expect, follow one of the two Forestry Commission trails described here in detail. Mountain bikers who want more to play with should veer off the fire road onto the Jeremy Cole MTB Trail (p89) to discover a maze of criss-crossing singletrack on a satisfying mix of gradients with the odd bomb hole thrown in to boot.

What is Friston's secret? Of course, there are eye-catching views and the sea air but there must be something more. Maybe it's the background chorus of forest birds or the leaves rustling. Whatever it is, it's hard not to come away feeling relaxed, refreshed and invigorated.

The family trail isn't the easiest riding on offer but it's manageable for active families and the forest environment more than makes up for any grumbling about the gradients. Forestry Commission trail map available at Seven Sisters Cycle shop.

S Near the entrance to the car park, follow the public bridleway to Westdean, along the side of the wooden fence. Ride **SA** for the Family Cycle Trail. Follow the green signs to ride along this wide, muddy track through the forest. There are some downhill sections and the ground can be uneven in places. It will be muddy when wet!

Pass the pond on your left and go through the gap beside the wall. Join the track in front of the house and continue **SA**. Pass the very, very long flight of woodland steps disappearing up towards Cuckmere Haven on your right. Follow the hard-surfaced stone and mud track on through the forest. It's straight, level easy riding.

By the house, keep riding **SA**, passing to the right of the buildings. The path remains level, with a compacted sandy shingle surface. There's a gap both sides of the track enabling you to enjoy the views into the forest, the simple lines of tree after tree after tree. Birds sing as they hurry about their business and you can't help but relax. Red singletrack crosses the path. Ride past the red and white stripy poles, following the green sign **SA**.

2 By the house, families with smaller children who may be tiring are advised to turn around and retrace their tyre tracks, as the trail becomes more tricky from hereon.

To explore the forest at closer quarters, ride on, following the track **L** before the building. Ride the short distance up the slope and by the green sign (and before you reach the metal gate) turn **L**. Don't be put off by the uphill: it's short and the path soon levels out. This mud track leads you into the forest.

3 **Look out for the L turn**. This is easy to miss because (currently) the side facing you on the rectangular wooden sign is blank! There is a green bike on the other side but it's easy to miss. If you do miss it, you'll find yourself turning left onto the steep slope beside Friston Hill instead.

Ride **L** up the slope. You will soon see a green family trail sign and you will also soon be racing down instead of pedalling up this grass and mud track. After the final downhill, turn **R** when you hit the track junction. Cycle along this hard-surfaced, wide stony path. It's nice and easy to ride.

4 Go **L** at the green sign. You now have a VERY big hill to climb. The only consolation is that it's wide and hard-surfaced and if you decide to stop for a rest halfway up, there are some great views over the forest. Enjoy a welcome downhill stretch, following the green signs **SA**. Turn **L** at the green sign by the bench with the viewpoint over the trees. Go round the metal gate and swoop downhill. At the track (occasional cars), turn **R**. You are now back on your earlier path. Follow the green signs back through Westdean, re-tracing your tyre tracks to find the forest car park, bike hire, café and visitor centre.

9.3 JEREMY COLE MTB TRAIL

FOREST	COUNTRY PARK

GRADE: ✳ ✳ ✳

DISTANCE: 11km / 7 miles

MAPS: OS Explorer 123; route waymarked; trail maps at car parks and at Seven Sisters Cycle shop.

The Jeremy Cole Mountain Bike Trail is a more demanding circuit. It's a red-graded forestry commission trail, which means that it's suitable for proficient mountain bikers with better quality off-road mountain bikes and good off-road riding skills. An added bonus regarding the Jeremy Cole Trail is, that unlike somewhere like Bedgebury, this trail's all natural!

We were a little disappointed with this one at first. Friston Hill is stunning but we were climbing with our backs to the view under a hot sun with no sign of a downhill stretch. Gradually, the paths begin to twist through the trees and suddenly, at Snap Hill, the views open out and you're taken along a steady woodland downhill run. From there on the route is varied and interesting, with a good mix of surfaces, tracks and gradients. It's far from easy and you'll be pleased with yourselves when you reach the end, but it's well worth the effort. It felt like more than seven miles to us but maybe that's just because we rode it straight after an almost lazy holiday!

This is Friston Forest at it's best: it's a great way to get off the beaten track. We did it on a bank holiday and saw only one or two cyclists. When we emerged at the Visitor Centre, the place was swarming with people and bikes.

I recommend starting from the Butchershole Car Park because it gives you an excuse to stop at the tea shop and means you ride the toughest part of the circuit first. It's equally possible, of course to do the whole circuit before you stop for tea and cake! The route is waymarked, although signposts could be clearer at times.

PARKING
BUTCHERSHOLE CAR PARK (see map p86)
From the A259, at Friston, take a **L** onto
Jevington Road. Butchershole Car Park is
on the **L** before you reach Jevington. **Note
closing time for car park on gate!**

ALTERNATIVE PARKING
Exceat Visitor Centre.

FAMILY RIDING
Only for older kids who are confident on
mountain bikes. The uphills make it tough,
and there are some tricky sections needing
careful supervision, but if they can cope
with it, it's fun.

S From Butchershole Car Park, follow the wooden sign for the MTB trail, heading **L** out of the car park. A wooden post signs you **L** for the *Jeremy Cole MTB Trail*. Follow the red arrow **SA** where the walking trail veers right. Ride on into leafy Friston Forest. Go through some wooden markers and turn **R** onto a small tarmac lane, where you may meet occasional forest traffic. Cycle up the hill and follow the track as it turns **L**.

2 At the wooden fence and waymarker no 17, ride (or push!) **R** up the hill towards Westdean. At the top of the slope, views open out onto Friston Hill to your right. Keep riding **SA**. As you come back into the woods, look out for the marker post showing you the track leading **R** into the woods.

3 Follow it! Cycle down the steep hill. You may want to control your speed as there's a huge patch of nettles at the bottom. I wouldn't want to land in it. Turn **R** onto the grassy bridleway, passing the marker post. This track climbs steadily... At the end, ignore the turn-off to the left and continue to follow path where it bends **L**. Ride on and up the slope. Follow the marker post and path **R** as you join another path. Soon, join a wider, grassy bridleway. Ride **L**, following the marker post. Where the path starts to descend, resist the downhill and go **R** instead at the all-too-easy-to-ignore post. I'm afraid there's a little bit more climbing: the track snakes upwards, fairly steeply. You may be beginning to feel like a downhill run's overdue and if you want to push, don't worry – the next path's more level and then there's one last climb... At the top of the slope turn **L** at the marker post. Ride on. Cross the stony track to turn **L** onto the narrow bridleway in front of you and keep pedalling.

4 At the top, follow the path **L** and almost immediately come to a marker post. Go **R** through the trees. Follow the path round the hollow. Note the red marker post. Keep following your nose even it feels like you're doubling back: this is a small loop. At the second marker post, turn **R** to complete this small loop and return to the main MTB trail.

Enjoy the down, yes, downhill return run through the woods. Emerge at the start of the loop. Turn **L** to return to the lower marker post at the start of the loop and then **R** to cycle along the narrow bridleway. Enjoy this fast grassy downhill. At the end, turn **R**, heading uphill again. Climb **R** towards Snap Hill. The great thing is you're about as high as you're going to go and you will soon be rewarded for all that climbing. There's a good long downhill stretch now, following the marker posts along a fairly obvious trail. Enjoy!

Ride along the crest of the hill. Fantastic views over the forest are all the more appreciated because they're sudden and unexpected. And you're still going downhill... Cross the stony bridleway (which forms part of the Family Trail). Go **SA** into the woods, following the red marker post. You may want to veer left if you prefer a more level track: lots of roots and bumps hereabout. Cross the path and continue into the woods opposite. Enjoy a gentle downhill on this windy and bumpy track through slightly more heathy terrain. Cross two gravel paths and follow the red marker up into the woods **SA**. Follow the track **L** and up, yes, up through the trees. It's steep! Notice spray paint directions on trees and avoid a wrong turn here.

5 At the top, turn **R**, following the wooden marker post. Enjoy a smoother ride, crossing a stone path briefly. Continue through the trees: you will spot red wooden markers. When you're riding parallel to the road on a slight downhill, look out for the unexpected **R** turn. Ride on and you should see a sign for *Exceat Car Park*. Lift your bike over the flint wall and enjoy the run. Keep an eye out for walkers and others as this area can be busy. Watch out for the second flint wall! Head downhill through the trees and you will emerge at Exceat car park.

6 You're at Exceat! You might want to stop at the tearoom, visit the Visitor Centre or search out the ice cream van in the car park over the main road.

To find the Mountain Bike Trail from Exceat Car Park, follow the signs for *bike hire* up through the car park. The trail heads off up through the trees and is signed for the *MTB Trail* and *Westdean*.

Pass your bike over two flint walls. At the top, ride **SA** following the track through the woods. After a steep little curve in the track you hit the bridleway which runs parallel with the road. Where there are two marker posts, turn **R**. To my mind, this is the trickiest stretch of path. I almost came off twice but perhaps that's just me! It's very narrow with some steep gradients, berms, uneven camber and lots of lovely slippery roots. Emerge back onto the bridleway and ride **L**. Ride across a shingle bridleway (or a quick **L** and then a **R** if you want to be pedantic), passing the red marker post to follow a narrow MTB track. Keep **SA** at the next marker post and ride on along this narrow path.

Turn **R**, cycling down a steep path through the woods. Ride it at your own speed: there are some steep gradients and berms. At the bottom, turn **R** where you emerge onto the leafy bridleway, avoiding the sharp bank/drop opposite. Ride **SA** on this wide bridleway that runs through the treetops. Where the path curves a marker post signals you **L**. This is a **very steep drop** with bumps/technical features that I didn't want to examine too closely! Not everyone in our party wanted to ride it; one of our bikes somehow went down the slope on its own... if you don't want to ride it, there are plenty of alternative tracks down the hill. If you do want to ride it, hold on tight!

Ride **SA** on the gravel path, following the red marker post as the track heads into the woods. Turn **R** along the narrow track and ride up a slight hill. The track curves round to the left and is signed by the marker post. Turn **L** onto a wide bridleway, following the red and green signs for a short way. Turn **R** at the next marker post, riding up through the trees. You are now back on the bridleway coming from Butchershole. If you are returning to the car park at Butchershole, turn **R** towards Friston Hill.

If you started at Exceat and want to complete the MTB Trail, ride **SA** and read from point 3 above.

Otherwise, ride down Friston Hill and turn **L** after the wooden gate. Curve round onto the tarmac lane and go **R**, passing between the wooden posts and cycle back to the car park.

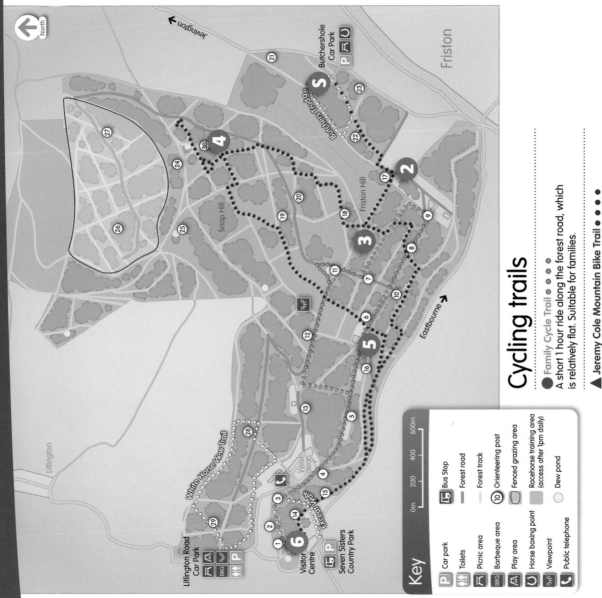

Cycling trails

Family Cycle Trail ● ● ●
A short 1 hour ride along the forest road, which is relatively flat. Suitable for families.

Jeremy Cole Mountain Bike Trail ● ● ●
A 7 mile undulating single track. For experienced riders.

Key

P Car park	Bus Stop
Toilets	Forest road
Picnic area	Forest track
BBQ Barbeque area	⑩ Orienteering post
Play area	Fenced grazing area
Horse boxing point	Racehorse training area (access after 1pm daily)
Viewpoint	Dew pond
Public telephone	

0m   200   400   600m

MAP REPRODUCED WITH KIND PERMISSION FROM THE FORESTRY COMMISSION

10 RYE HARBOUR NATURE RESERVE LOOP
including Cadborough Cliff & Camber Castle

TOURIST TRAIL

GRADE: *

DISTANCE: 9km / 5.5 miles

MAPS: OS Explorer 125

This route follows NCR 2 along a stunning off-road track out of Rye, beneath Cadborough Cliff. After a short road link through Winchelsea, we return across fields on a bridleway which runs alongside the River Brede, passing military defence ruins and Camber Castle. This bridleway is definitely 'off-road' and could be muddy.

Take the optional route down to Winchelsea Beach/Rye Harbour and explore Rye Harbour Nature Reserve. This runs on hard surfaces.

LINKS WITH
NCR 2 – from Rye, ride on, following the NCR 2 towards Lyd, passing beautiful Camber Sands beach.

EASY ACCESS
No, but Rye Harbour Nature Reserve is an ideal place for visitors with limited mobility because the ground is level and most footpaths have a good surface. There is a private road that runs through the Beach Reserve that is good for wheelchairs and all four birdwatching hides are accessible to some wheelchairs.

PUBLIC TRANSPORT
TRAIN STATION: **Rye.**

PARKING
WINCHELSEA ROAD
(Cheap!)

WISH STREET
Pay and Display (height barrier)

GIBBET MARSH, UDIMORE ROAD
Long stay car park

RYE HARBOUR

BIKE HIRE
RYE HIRE LTD, CYPRUS PLACE
T 01797 223 033
www.ryehire.co.uk

FOOD, DRINK AND ACCOMMODATION
No specific suggestions but try
www.visitrye.co.uk or
www.ukcampsite.co.uk

There are several campsites in the area and a good choice of accommodation.

WILLIAM THE CONQUEROR
Recently refurbished and by the river, a Shepherd Neame pub.
T 01797 223 315
www.williamtheconqueror.co.uk

THE OLD VICARAGE B&B, RYE HARBOUR
See website for details of cycling storage.
T 01797 222 088
www.oldvicarageryeharbour.co.uk

SHERI'S CAFE, HARBOUR ROAD, RYE HARBOUR
Don't be put off by the portable cabin. Good value, recommended basic grub.

THE INKERMAN ARMS
Welcoming. Home-cooked food every day until 8pm (6pm on Sundays).
T 01797 222 464

POSSIBLE PICNIC SPOTS
ROYAL MILITARY CANAL
A footpath (Saxon Shore Way) gives access to the banks of the Royal Military Canal at Winchelsea.

THE BEACH!

POINTS OF INTEREST
RYE HARBOUR NATURE RESERVE
Rye Harbour is best known for the Little Tern, although sadly in very recent years the bird has failed to breed here. Shingle habitat is very rare in Europe and together with Dungeness, Rye Bay forms the largest coastal shingle feature in Europe. Wildlife that exists on shingle survives in a harsh environment and as you explore the nature reserve, the bleak, wide open seascape surrounds you.
www.wildrye.info

Rye Harbour is witness to the interaction between man, nature and landscape. Historical military defences such as Camber Castle sit amid gravel ridges, island nesting birds flock to the saline lagoons in the old industrial gravel pits and a surprising number of species thrive in the salt marshes and on the shingle. To find out more, visit Lime Kiln Cottage Information Centre.

FAMILY RIDING
Yes, if they're road-happy enough to manage the link through Winchelsea. The first section beneath Cadborough Cliff is an ideal family ride.

TO GET TO THE START

From Winchelsea Road (A259), look for a footpath between the row of terrace houses and the bridge on the garage side of the river. Push your bike through several gates and across the railway line as you travel along this footpath next to the river. Emerge in a grassy area to pick up the NCR 2.

Or, from Gibbet Marsh car park, cycle towards the windmill to pick up the NCR 2.

S Start at the green cycle marker post in the corner of the field. Head **L** towards Camber, and Rye town centre. Ride over a wooden bridge, following the blue NCR 2 sign. Go over a second bridge to follow the path **R**. Ride through wooden posts and turn **L**, still following the NCR 2 sign. As you ride along these easy bridleways, enjoy Cadborough Cliff to your right and open views across Rye Marsh to your left. It's beautiful. Pass through metal gates and ride on. Pass through another gate. Ride over a cattle grid, keeping an eye out for that blue NCR 2 sign.

2 Ride **SA** onto the lane. At the end of Dumb Woman's Lane, ride **L** towards Winchelsea, following NCR 2. Cross the open railway crossing with care, passing Winchelsea's small station. Follow the road around, crossing a small river. The lane follows the river as you approach the outskirts of Winchelsea. Pass Ferryfields Holiday Home Park.

3 At the next junction turn **L**, joining the busy A259 on a downhill hairpin bend. Thankfully, a cycle path is signed along the pavement, as this stretch of road is fast and narrow. Ride into Winchelsea, passing The Bridge Inn.

4 Turn **R** just after the pub. Ride towards Winchelsea Beach, following the NCR 2 sign. See the Royal Military Canal on your right. You are now cycling on quieter roads. Pass Sutton's Fish and Game shop and ride on.

5 At the corner, with the black and white 'sharp bend' signs, leave the road, going **SA** to follow the bridleway down the private road.

OPTIONAL ROUTE TO THE SEA AND RYE HARBOUR NATURE RESERVE

Continue around the sharp bend along Sea Road. Pass the Ship Inn on your left and Pub 31 on your right. Turn **L** along Dogshill Road. Pass a playground on your left and ride on. Reach the seafront where there's a small car park and public toilet. If you wish to leave your bikes and walk through the reserve, turn **L**. There's a narrow track beside the beach and a wide tarmac lane. The Environment Agency do not allow cycling because the tarmac paths are used by heavy traffic to move shingle, especially in winter. A flying flag at the Rye Harbour end indicates that lorries are working. At the end of the tarmac lane, turn **L** to visit Lime Kiln Cottage Information Centre.

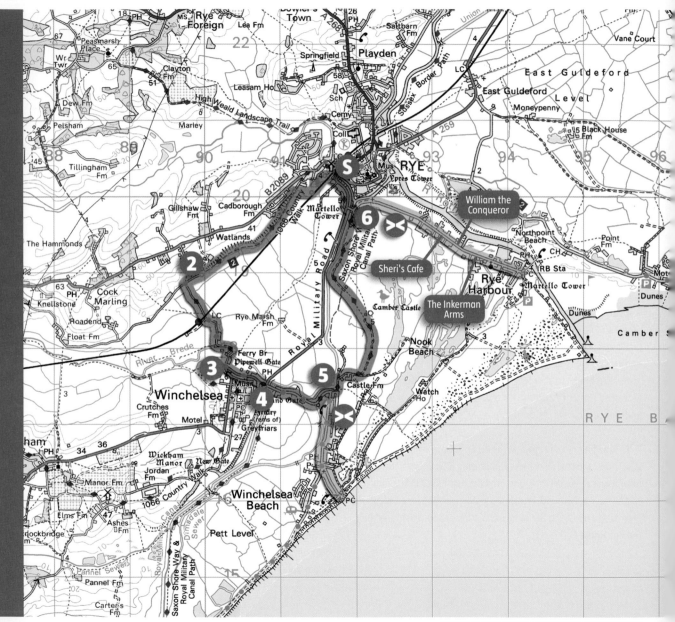

Ride along the private road – a tarmac lane. Where the lane bends, leave it and follow the bridleway through the River Brede Farm and Campsite. Ride **SA**. Just before you come to the sewage works, turn **L** through the metal gates onto the bridleway. The path is grassy, rough and not initially obvious. Follow your nose, preferably away from the sewage works. This bridleway could be hard-going when wet but it is in a great location: it runs between the River Brede and a reed bed with Camber Castle to the right. Surely there must be a few water voles busy in that reed bed?

Where the mud track forks, keep **R** to stay on the bridleway. If you would like a closer look at Camber Castle, the Saxon Shore Way footpath leads off to the right. Follow the reed bed round until you come to the bank next to the River Breed. Ride on. Go through the gate and keep right to stay on the bridleway. Rye is one mile away!

6 When you reach the road, you have a choice:
TO RETURN TO RYE

Turn **L** and ride across the bridge over the River Brede. At the end of Harbour Road, turn **R**. Ride this unavoidable, but short, busy section of the A259, with a pavement running alongside. If you wish to return to the start point from Winchelsea Road, look for a footpath between the terrace of houses and the bridge on the garage side of the river. Push your bike through several gates and across the railway line as you travel along this footpath next to the river. Emerge beside the windmill and the NCR 2 marker of our start point.

OPTIONAL ROUTE TO RYE HARBOUR

If you haven't already done so, why not turn **R** along Harbour Road to visit Rye Harbour and Rye Harbour Nature Reserve? There's a clue in the name of the road and the first two thirds are fairly industrial in nature but luckily, a cycle path runs alongside the pavement as far as the church and small play area. Pass The Inkerman Arms on your right. At the harbour, there's a café or two and the William the Conqueror pub has a terrace that overlooks the boats. You may wish to leave your bikes and explore Rye Harbour Nature Reserve too. It's well worth the effort for the sea air alone!

west sussex

west sussex

PORTSMOUTH to	
Bilbao	29-35 hrs
Caen	6-7 hrs
Guernsey	7 hrs
Jersey	11 hrs
Le Havre	8 hrs
St Malo	11 hrs

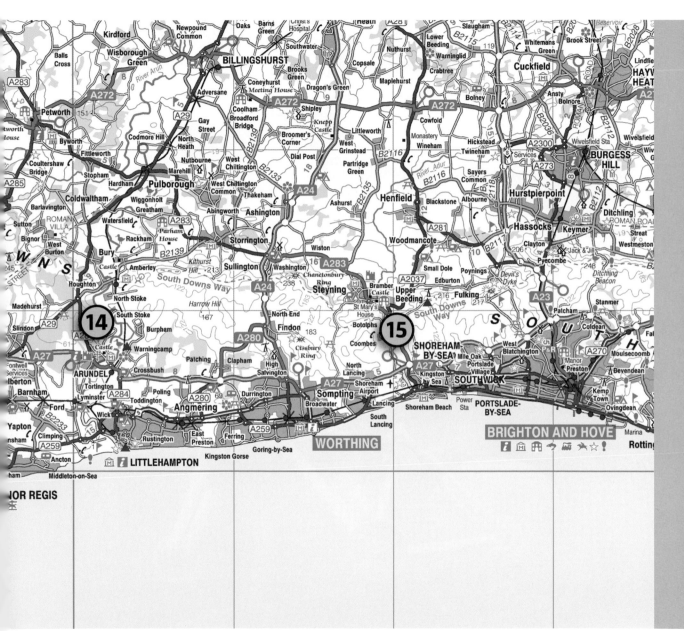

11 CENTURION WAY
Chichester to West Dean

CYCLEWAY

GRADE: ✳

DISTANCE: 8.8km / 5.5 miles (linear)

MAPS: OS Explorer 120; Council Map

It's surprising how quickly a bicycle can whizz you out of a busy town and into agricultural Sussex. This cycleway was extended to West Dean in 2002 and serves as a link between Chichester and the rural villages. A local schoolboy named it Centurion Way because a Roman road crosses the path near Lavant.

It has so much more to offer than just an easy ride: a nature reserve, sculptures, an adventure playground and a good spot to end up at! West Dean nestles in the River Lavant valley and boasts flint houses, riverside picnic spots, a friendly pub and welcoming cafe with seating for all weathers.

LINKS WITH
Salterns Way, Bill Way, Sustrans Regional Route 88, Sustrans NCR 2. Or try the strenuous bridleway climb past the Arboretum and then down Town Lane to Singleton.

EASY ACCESS
See point 4. See *www.visitsouthdowns.com* section on Easy Access Trails for more information. There's a gate at each end of this 1.5km path, which runs from West Dean Estate towards Chichester. At the Binderton House end, there's a bus stop but there's also a steep slope down from the A286. Views over Sussex farmland lead your eye past flint houses towards the Downs along my favourite section of the Centurion Way. Brandy Hole Copse is unsuitable for wheelchair users.

PUBLIC TRANSPORT
TRAIN STATIONS: Chichester, Fishbourne.
BUS: Stagecoach bus stop: outside Selsey Arms.

PARKING
FOR EASY ACCESS SECTION
Lavant Down Road is off the A286, Midhurst Road in Mid Lavant. The other end is also off the A286, towards West Dean. The trail is situated on the right just before Binderton House but you must go down a slope to reach it.

CHICHESTER
To get to start: Driving west on the A27 round Chichester, take the A259 (dual carriageway) into Chichester just before the A27 veers off towards Havant. Continue across the railway line to the Westbourne Link Roundabout

where you turn **L**. Drive **L** again into Westgate. Continue until you see the school entrance on your right and space to park on your left. On weekdays, after joining the A259, turn **L** into Fishbourne Road, past the Tesco and garage. Continue round until you park. From Fishbourne Road, double back on your bike, following the cycle path across the level crossing and go **L** past the house.

ALTERNATIVE START: WEST DEAN
Drive down the lane beside the Selsey Arms and turn **R** to park on the grass and shingle side.

BIKE HIRE
BLACK POINT CYCLE HIRE
Located by Sandy Point on Hayling Island but they will deliver within a radius of 20 miles.
www.haylingbikehire.co.uk

HARGROVES CYCLES, CHICHESTER
T 01243 537 337
www.hargrovescycles.co.uk/stores-chichester

CITY CYCLES, CHICHESTER
T 01243 539 992
www.citycycleschichester.co.uk

GEARED BIKES, CHICHESTER
South of the A27 towards West Wittering.
T 01243 784 479
www.gearedbikes.co.uk

FOOD AND DRINK
PUB / 4* B&B
THE DEAN ALE AND CIDER HOUSE
Formerly The Selsey Arms, now refurbished

to its country inn roots. New restaurant area, large courtyard and allocated parking for bicycles.
T 01243 811 465
http://thedeaninn.co.uk

WEST DEAN STORES & CAFE
Supplies! Teas, coffees, baps, cream teas, and ice cream. Open daily until 6.30 pm, 1 pm on Sunday.
T 01243 818 163
www.westdeanstores.co.uk

ACCOMMODATION
CHILGROVE FARM B&B
This 4* B&B nestles beneath the South Downs in an Area of Natural Beauty, approximately 3 miles from Lavant. There are places where bikes could be locked up outside but if you really can't bear to be parted from it, they'll let you have it in your en suite room!
T 01243 519 436
www.chilgrovefarmbedandbreakfast.co.uk

POINTS OF INTEREST
BRANDY HOLE COPSE
This nature reserve is 15 acres of old coppice and mixed woodland, including ponds and, perhaps incongruously, old WW2 anti-tank defences. Local rumour has it that a barrel of brandy was found hidden in a smuggler's cave when the railway line was being built. Hence, the name!
www.brandyholecopse.org.uk

FAMILY RIDING
Perfect for a family ride, some steep hills near the end but fairly short-lived.

S Ride up the path to the right of the house towards Bishop Luffa School. At the school gates, turn **L** through the metal barriers. This is the start of Centurion Way. Pass beneath the 'Roman Archway' and continue **SA**.

The first section of the trail leads you out of Chichester on the line of the old railway. There's a slight uphill gradient but the tarmac surface makes for such easy riding that you will barely notice it. There are various access points along this stretch and the path is well-used by local residents. Ride on.

2 Before too long you'll reach a turning before a railway bridge. There's a sculpture of an angel riding a horse towards a nature reserve. Turn off to cycle towards Brandy Hole Copse where you may padlock your bike (anchor points on bridge?) and explore on foot.

Enjoy the smooth downhill then there's perhaps a bit of a climb for kids but it's worth it because when you reach the top, the views open out and it's a perfect spot to linger. Some may choose to relax on a couple of broad sleepers while others investigate the roman centurion sculptures a.k.a. *The Chichester Road Gang*. There's also a sculpture called *The Roman Amphitheatre* away to the left. Can you spot it?

Here Centurion Way is also part of Sustrans National Cycle Route 88. Follow the sign to *Lavant*, through the brick bridge. Keep riding **SA** to West Dean/Singleton. You can't miss the 'Primary Hanger' sculptures as you cycle under the railway bridge.

Continue on past the back of some flats in the building that has done time as Lavant Station.

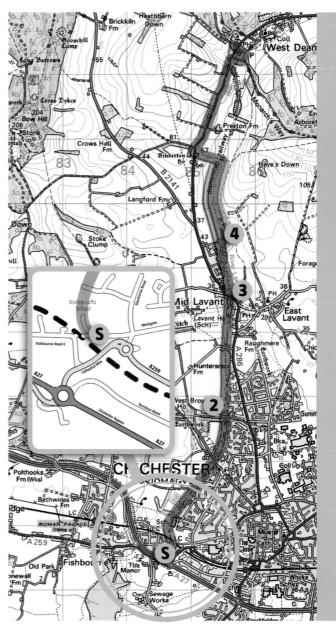

3 At the sign to *Warbleheath Close*, turn **R** to join the road ahead. Families with children may want to take a break at Churchmead Children's Play Area. This grassy park is tucked away on the site of the old railway line and includes wooden adventure playthings such as a short towrope.

Cycle the short distance to the end of Churchmead Close. Turn **R** following the blue cycle sign towards West Dean. Go through the concrete bollards and, following the blue sticker sign on the lamp post, ride **SA** through the residential area. Spot another blue sign on a lamp post and take a **R** turn at the grassy roundabout, heading towards the path in the far corner.

4 Here, Centurion Way starts again, following the path of the old railway line. *[Easy Access section]* This is an easy riding track with a level surface of fine shingle which turns to level compacted mud. This is my favourite section of the cycleway, perhaps because the views suddenly open out over arable farmland towards the edge of the Downs. At the wooden waymarker where the track joins the bridleway, cycle **SA**. Pass through the wooden gate. You are leaving Centurion Way.

Ride **SA** up a short but nasty hill towards the A286. No need to cycle on the road: there's a cycle path. Follow the cycle path **R** towards the bus stop, passing a slightly hidden wooden waymarker. Ride this undulating tarmac cycle path, crossing the entrance to Farbridge Conference Centre with care. Continue on this nice 'n easy surface until you approach down the hill to West Dean. The path narrows at a nasty spot in the road so there's a 'cyclists dismount/ red tarmac' section. Sweep downhill to the end of the cycleway at the wooden waymarker.

Turn **R** along the small lane that circles round the back of the village. Cycle it to find a grassy bank by a shallow stream and a couple of pretty bridges where you may rest or picnic. To reach West Dean Stores or the Selsey Arms, turn **L** past the flint house and cycle up the short lane.

12 SALTERNS WAY & BOSHAM PENINSULAR CIRCUIT

CYCLEWAY   TOURIST TRAIL

GRADE: *

DISTANCE: 18km / 11 miles + return loop (6.5km / 4 miles)

MAPS: OS Explorer 120; Chichester Harbour Conservancy Map

This route combines some of the best things in life: fast, easy cycling; good food, sea air, the sound of yachts clinking, a sandy beach, and even the chance to embark upon a small passenger ferry. What more could you want?

Salterns Way is an 18km cycle route linking Chichester Cathedral with the sand dunes of East Head. En route, you'll cycle along easy cycle paths through crop farms and round fields on this agricultural peninsular and you'll spin down quiet lanes which are home to an eclectic mix of houses. Salterns Way has been funded by the Heritage Lottery Fund and is managed by Chichester Harbour Conservancy.

We're including an additional section, suggested by a local bike shop owner, in which you jump on a passenger ferry, bike 'n all, and whiz back along the quiet lanes of the Bosham Peninsular to Chichester. There's an added bonus with this loop: there's a definite downhill feel to some sections but the uphill that you're waiting for never comes. I don't know how it works, but I like it.

LINKS WITH
Centurion Way, Bill Way, Sustrans Regional
Route 88.

EASY ACCESS
Several off-road sections of Salterns Way –
highlighted on the map in red and green –
should offer access opportunities for
all-terrain or soft-wheeled wheelchairs.
See the *Access For All* section at
www.conservancy.co.uk for more information.

DEVELOPMENT
None planned.

PUBLIC TRANSPORT
TRAIN STATIONS: Chichester, Bosham.

PARKING
CHICHESTER
Various, or see start of **Bill Way/Centurion
Way** routes.

DELL QUAY
Follow signs for *Dell Quay* off the A286,
driving along Dell Quay Road. Busy at
weekends.

CHICHESTER MARINA
Free visitor car park.

WEST WITTERING BEACH CAR PARK

PUBLIC TOILETS
Chichester Marina.
West Wittering Beach Car Park.

BIKE HIRE
BLACK POINT CYCLE HIRE
Located by Sandy Point on Hayling Island but
they will deliver within a radius of 20 miles.
www.haylingbikehire.co.uk

HARGROVES CYCLES, CHICHESTER
T 01243 537 337
www.hargrovescycles.co.uk/stores-chichester

CITY CYCLES, CHICHESTER
T 01243 539 992
www.citycycleschichester.co.uk

BARREG BIKES, ON THE A259 AT FISHBOURNE
T 01243 786 104
www.barreg.co.uk

FOOD AND DRINK
DELL QUAY – CROWN & ANCHOR
This pub has fresh fish delivered daily!
Fish battered in Youngs Real Ale is the most
popular dish from their substantial menu
but they also offer cooked breakfasts and
lighter snacks from their outdoor 'terrace'
kitchen. Its outstanding location, overlooking
Dell Quay, makes it doubly popular so
booking is advisable. Children welcome.
T 01243 781 712
www.crownandanchorchichester.com

THE BOAT HOUSE CAFÉ
Good views of the harbour. Breakfasts,
snacks, light meals and bistro dinner menu.
T 01243 513 203
*www.idealcollection.co.uk/
theboathousecafe-chichester*

THE LAMB INN
A short diversion from our route along
a busy road to this tile hung real ale pub
with garden.
T 01243 511 105
www.thelambwittering.co.uk

WEST WITTERING – BEACH HOUSE CAFÉ
Guest house and B&B with licensed
restaurant. Country Stores: picnic hampers,
tea and coffee to go.
T 01243 514 800
www.beachhse.co.uk

THE LANDING CAFE, POUND ROAD
Near the entrance to West Wittering Estate.
T 01243 513 757

ITCHENOR – ITCHENOR SHIP INN
Traditional pub food, fresh local fish,
open all day with a terrace at the front.
Accommodation available.
T 01243 512 284
www.theshipinnitchenor.co.uk

ACCOMMODATION
EAST WITTERING – STUBCROFT FARM CAMPSITE
Stubcroft Farm Campsite is tucked away on
a working sheep farm close to sandy beaches

and Chichester Harbour. The campsite is family friendly with an emphasis on sustainability and wildlife conservation.
www.stubcroft.com

CAMP SITES

THE WALNUT TREE CARAVAN PARK
T 01243 670 207
www.islandmeadow.co.uk

NUNNINGTON FARM CARAVAN AND CAMPING SITE
T 01243 514 013
www.camping-in-sussex.com

BOAT TRIPS

ITCHENOR – BOSHAM PASSENGER FERRY
Across the Chichester Channel. Bikes welcome!
T 07970 378 350
www.itchenorferry.co.uk

CHICHESTER HARBOUR WATER TOURS
See wildlife in a variety of habitats.
1½ hour trips from Itchenor.
T 01243 670 504
www.chichesterharbourwatertours.co.uk

WATER SPORTS

WEST WITTERING BEACH – WATERSPORTS CLUB, HIRE & TUITION
T 01243 513 077
www.2xs.co.uk

POINTS OF INTEREST

CHICHESTER HARBOUR CONSERVANCY:
Dell Quay is an Area of Outstanding Natural Beauty where the mudflats play host to a variety of nature and wildlife.
www.conservancy.co.uk

FAMILY RIDING

If you would prefer a shorter route or an idea for a ride with older, road-safe children and teenagers, then park at West Wittering Beach and head back along the mainly quiet roads (one or two uphills) and off-road easy paths towards Chichester Marina, where they serve delicious burgers. You can cycle back fast and enjoy a well-deserved sunbathe on the soft sand, or a swim in the sea.

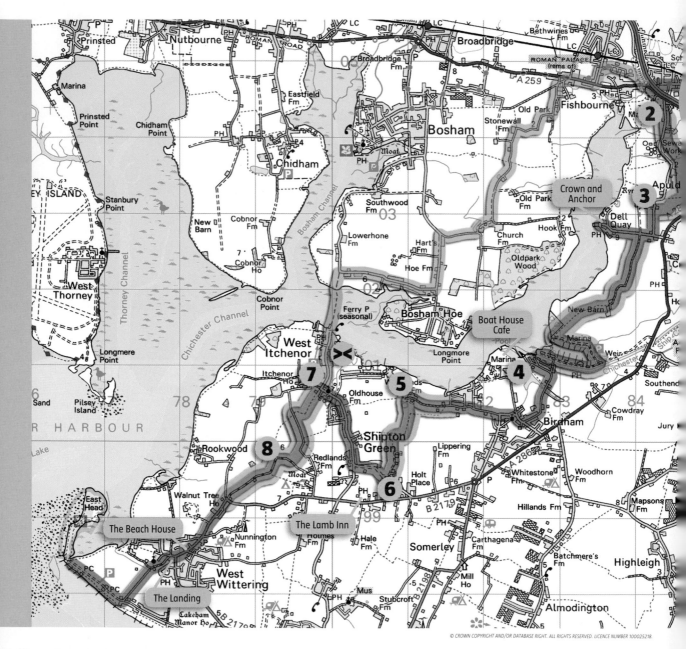

© CROWN COPYRIGHT AND/OR DATABASE RIGHT. ALL RIGHTS RESERVED. LICENCE NUMBER 100025218.

S Salterns Way route starts at The Cross. This busy intersection is in the main shopping area of Chichester where North, South, East and West Streets all converge. Cycle along West Street. This section is for road-happy cyclists only. It leads you past Chichester Cathedral. At the roundabout go **SA**, taking the 2nd exit, cycling into historic, red brick Westgate. *No. 12* wine bar is on the corner. Cycle on along Westgate. Notice the lane which links to Chichester station on your left. Keep riding, going **SA** at the roundabout.

Pass the entrance to Bishop Luffa school and the start point for the Centurion Way (p105). Follow the sign for Fishbourne, and cross the railway crossing and follow the road **SA**. Keep going until you pass under a bridge. Follow the blue sign for Fishbourne and Bosham.

After the bridge, there's a short, optional diversion to Fishbourne Roman Palace, following Emperor Way Cycle and Pedestrian Track **R**. If you're following our loop, you will come back past it as you return to the city. It's under cover so you won't see much unless you pay to go in.

Go **L** along a short, tarmac cycle path. Avoid cycling on this busy 'A' road by crossing at the traffic island and joining the tarmac shared-use path on the opposite side of the road. Turn **R** into Appledram Lane (South), following signs for Dell Quay and Apuldram.

2 After the farm buildings, go through a wooden kissing gate to take the permissive cycleway. This is Salterns Way Cycle and Wheelchair Path. It follows the edge of the field, running adjacent to the road. Crop-pickers were enjoying a quick lunch break when I cycled through here. Chichester Cathedral spire is clearly visible to your left. Cross the bridge and the path veers left away from the road through more fields. Pass the back of the

Apuldram Centre. Go through an opening into another field. Turn **R** as the cycleway joins a public footpath. This whole section is fantastic with great views and easy riding.

3 Turn **L** where the route rejoins Appledram Lane. Cycle **R** at the junction with Dell Lane. Ride a short way. If you wish to visit the Crown and Anchor or Dell Quay itself, continue **SA**.

To continue on Salterns Way, turn **L** at the wooden waymarker. There's a small white *Salterns Way* sign and a sign for *Apuldram Manor Farm*. Cycle on, continuing through the farm buildings, following occasional white marker posts. There are views of yacht masts at Dell Quay and distant downland to your right.

The path narrows as you go through Salterns Wood Copse, one of the few remaining areas of woodland around Chichester Harbour. Look out for birds such as the Black Cap and Great Spotted Woodpecker. The path emerges at Chichester Marina. This could be a good place to stop for a rest or a picnic: there's a wall you can sit on to watch the boats. Go **L** and cycle around Chichester Marina, through car parks and along the road. At the end, go around the road barrier. Turn **R**. You are cycling between Chichester Canal and the Harbour Centre. Head **R** to visit *The Spinnaker* or *Four Seasons Country Store*.

See the houseboats along the canal. Pass historic Egremont Bridge. Cycle up the path to the left of Chichester Yacht Club. At the end, you must dismount to cross the footbridge across the lock. Push your bike along the footpath **SA** and then **R** at the brick wall, crossing in front of the gateposts. Continue until the end of a short gravel footpath.

4 Turn **L** onto the lane, following the white Salterns Way markers. Ride on. This is Lock Lane. It's very quiet but you may meet the odd car. It becomes Broomers Lane and then Martins Lane. Come to a junction with Church Lane (fast, occasional cars!). Pass St James Church, Birdham on your left. Keep going **SA** at the junction. Enjoy this gentle downhill. Pass Westlands to your right. Keep cycling past Ham Lodge and Westland Farm as the lane changes into a concrete track. See the yacht masts bobbing on your right.

5 Before you reach the big barns, come to a double gatepost on your left. Go through the kissing gate and follow Salterns Way **L** on the sandy mud path. This is another section of the Salterns Way Cycle and Wheelchair Path. It's not as level as the previous section but easily negotiable.

Go round the whole field, sticking to the Salterns Way. Enter a second field. As you approach the footpath to the caravan park, go **R** through a gate following a Salterns Way sign. Cycle **L** along a track. Keep **SA** along the edge of a field, passing another entrance to the caravan park. Go through a gate to leave this section of off-road track.

6 Turn **R** and cycle on. Ignore the left turn signed for the Witterings and follow the small Salterns Way marker post as the road curves right. There are some downhill stretches and a lot of appealing houses to look at. Pass Itchenor Village Pond and St Nicholas Church.

7 At the next corner, where the road curves right and passes the entrance to Itchenor Park House, you have a choice:

OPTIONAL RETURN LOOP VIA ITCHENOR:

To follow our extra loop back via Itchenor and the foot passenger ferry to Chichester, stay on the road into Itchenor. Ride on. Head past the Harbour Office and out along the slipway to catch the small Itchenor Passenger Ferry across Chichester Channel. It's only a short journey but it's great to rest your legs and be out on the water. The ferryman will help you lift your bikes on and off shore: not quite so easy when you land at Smugglers Lane. There's been a ferry crossing here since the 17th century and you do almost feel like you're being put ashore on a wild coastline. Not for long though: this is the South East!

Follow the gravel footpath the short distance to the small car park. There are bike posts here if you're cycling the other way and want to leave your bike.

Turn **R**. Ride round Hoe Lane until you come to a turn-off for Chichester and Fishbourne. Turn **R** here. Cycle on, ignoring the turn-off into Hook Lane. There are some fantastic views over open farmland and distant downland. Look out for Chichester Cathedral to the right. Cycle on, taking care where the road narrows.

As you come into the outskirts of Chichester, at the end of Old Park Lane, you hit a T-junction with a busy road. Turn **R**, riding on the red cyclepath.

Just past the bike shop, leave the road to go **L** along Legionary Trail. Turn **L** onto West View and R onto Roman Way, passing first the school and then Fishbourne Roman Villa along Emperor Way Cycle and Pedestrian Track. Turn **L**, retracing the start of the main route back to The Cross at the heart of Chichester.

Or, to ride to West Wittering Beach along the rest of Salterns Way, leave the road to head towards Itchenor Park House and Farm. Immediately head **L** before the driveway and then go **R** through the signed gate. You are now on another section of Salterns Way Cycle and Wheelchair Path. The track leads up and away between the trees and the fence. Cycle through Itchenor Meadow, which provides a valuable habitat to increase diversity of species such as butterflies and spiders. If you see teasels, you may spot a goldfinch nearby as it's a popular food source for them.

Follow this enjoyable mud track until you hit a concrete farm road. Turn **L** and follow this easy, wide path round. At the opening in the hedge, ride **R**. Cycle across the mud track at the end of a field of crops. Go through the wooden gate: this is the end of the Cycle and Wheelchair section.

8 Turn **R** along Sheepwash Lane. It looks like a bridleway but be warned, cars do use this path. Stay on Sheepwash Lane, ignoring any footpaths. You may start to feel a sea-breeze around this section of stony path. As you cycle through the fields under a hot sun, what could be better than knowing that one of the south's best sandy beaches is waiting for you?

Turn **R** onto Rook Wood Road. There's significant traffic especially in high season so take care. Continue past the small row of shops. Pass Walnut Tree Caravan Park on your right and Nunnington Farm Caravan and Camping Site on your left.

Cycle on through West Wittering, with its refined beach village resort atmosphere. Ignore two small closes on your right. At the brown sign for *West Wittering Beach*, turn **R** into Pound Road. Pass the public toilets and turn **L** into the car park for the beach. Cycle along the long drive, waving at queuing cars in summer. **Dismount** to go through the pay gate and enjoy the beach!

TO RETURN

Retrace your tyre tracks but remember, at point 7, you may wish to return to Chichester a different way by catching the Itchenor Passenger Ferry and riding along quiet country roads with the cathedral beckoning you back.

13 BILL WAY

CYCLEWAY   TOURIST TRAIL

GRADE: ✳

DISTANCE: 13km / 8 miles

MAPS: OS Explorer 120; Manhood Cycle Network guide (*www.manhoodcyclenetwork.org.uk*)

I was told about this new cycleway by a Chichester bike shop owner and I'm so glad that I didn't miss it! It's easy to ride with a good variety of terrain. There's something very satisfying about riding out of a city under your own steam and reaching wide-open spaces, fresh air and Sussex countryside.

Through a car window, you might not give some of these views over mainly flat land a second glance, but somehow, as you ride through this agricultural peninsula on two wheels, you become a part of the landscape and it becomes bigger and more awe-inspiring the further you go. Maybe it's the sea air or the feeling of space, but this peninsula ride certainly has a lot to offer.

It is due to the continuing hard work of a group of cyclists, the *Manhood Cycle Network,* that increasing numbers of us can enjoy these bike rides. Their vision and campaigning for safe cycle routes between all settlements on the Manhood Peninsula continues to make these routes enjoyable and accessible for more and more cyclists.

LINKS WITH
Centurion Way, Salterns Way, NCR 2,
Sustrans Route 88 for cyclists and walkers.
www.manhoodcyclenetwork.org.uk

EASY ACCESS
Yes, the canal towpath from the Canal Basin to
Hunston is well-maintained and certainly hard-
surfaced at the canal basin end. Those wanting
to explore further afield should investigate
the permissive pathways at point 3, which
are probably easy access in good conditions.

DEVELOPMENT
Proposed extension from Pagham Harbour
Nature Reserve to Selsey. Safer off-road cycle
path/road crossing from Ferry Corner to Golf
Links Lane.

PUBLIC TRANSPORT
TRAIN STATIONS: Chichester, Fishbourne.

PARKING
To get to the start: Driving west on the
A27 round Chichester, take the A259 (dual
carriageway) into Chichester just before
the A27 veers off towards Havant. Continue
across the railway line to the Westbourne
Link Roundabout where you turn **L**. Drive **L**
again into Westgate. Continue until you see
the Bishop Luffa School entrance on your
right and space to park on your left.
On weekdays, after joining the A259, turn
L into Fishbourne Road, past the Tesco and
garage. Continue round until you park.

AVENUES DE CHARTRES (WEST) CAR PARK
In front of Westgate Leisure Centre, Chichester.

MULTI-STOREY CAR PARK
Off the A259 Via Ravenna (height restrictions).

HUNSTON
Off the B2145, near the canal path.

BIKE HIRE
BLACK POINT CYCLE HIRE
Located by Sandy Point on Hayling Island but
they will deliver within a radius of 20 miles.
www.haylingbikehire.co.uk

BIKE SHOPS
BARREG CYCLES, FISHBOURNE
T 01243 786 104

HARGROVES CYCLES, CHICHESTER
T 01243 537 337
www.hargrovescycles.co.uk/stores-chichester

CITY CYCLES, CHICHESTER
T 01243 539 992
www.citycycleschichester.co.uk

GEARED BIKES, CHICHESTER
South of the A27 towards West Wittering.
T 01243 784 479
www.gearedbikes.co.uk

FOOD AND DRINK
Various options in Chichester:

CHICHESTER SHIP CANAL TRUST
Small café (cakes & tea) and shop.
T 01243 771 363
www.chichestercanal.org.uk

THE CRAB & LOBSTER, SIDLESHAM
More restaurant than pub, but for a light lunch
they will do sandwiches or a starter and chips.
Use local produce, with an emphasis on fresh
fish. Terrace and beer garden.
T 01243 641 233
www.crab-lobster.co.uk

IDEAL PICNIC SPOT
Benches overlooking Pagham Harbour at
Sidlesham Quay.

ACCOMMODATION
THE CRAB & LOBSTER, SIDLESHAM
Luxurious and comfortable en suite rooms
or self-catering cottage. A definite option
for a hideaway weekend.
T 01243 641 233
www.crab-lobster.co.uk

OLD CHAPEL FORGE BED & BREAKFAST
Cyclists welcome. Gold Award from
Green Tourism Business Scheme.
Luxury seventeenth-century boutique
accommodation in the heart of the South
Downs. Free pick-ups from local station,
laundry and drying facilities.
T 01243 264 380
M 07709 993 031
www.oldchapelforge.co.uk

POINTS OF INTEREST

CHICHESTER SHIP CANAL

Daily canal boat trips (wheelchair access available). Also, row boat hire, canoe day tickets, angling, Easter Bunny and Father Christmas boat trips.

T 01243 771 363 (same day bookings)
T 01243 377 405 (advance bookings)
www.chichestercanal.org.uk

PAGHAM HARBOUR LOCAL NATURE RESERVE

Bike racks, toilets. Pagham Harbour was probably in use as *Uedringmutha* harbour back in Saxon times and thrived during certain periods. However, by the 1870s trade declined, probably due to competition from the roads, and the harbour was reclaimed for agriculture. Nowadays, about half of this 1,450 acre reserve is intertidal salt marshes and mudflats supporting not only birds but a vast number of invertebrate animals. The rest is farmland, copses, lagoons, reedbeds and shingle beaches. The farmland is particularly valuable for feeding waders such as black-tailed godwits and curlews, and the shingle banks provide highly desirable residences for birds such as ringed plovers and oystercatchers. The Ferry Pool Lagoon is one of the top birdwatching sites in Sussex, especially during autumn migration when red-breasted mergansers may put in an appearance.
www.rspb.org.uk

FAMILY RIDING

Families would be best to start at the canal basin. Otherwise the route is suitable for children, providing they're happy to ride on the quiet lanes between North and South Mundham.

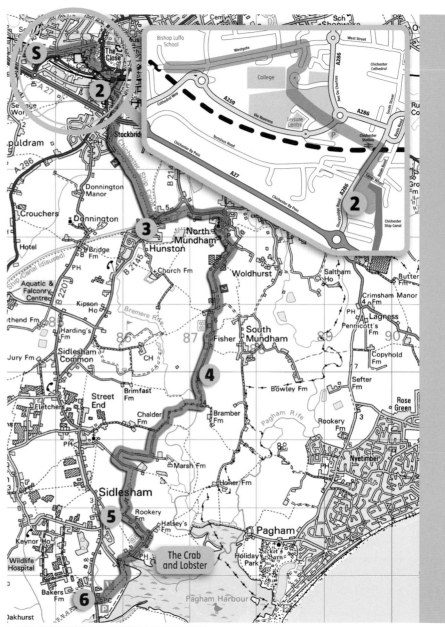

SI am starting route directions for the Bill Way by Bishop Luffa School, on Westgate in Chichester (PO19 3LT). This gives cyclists the opportunity to ride out from the centre of Chichester and to link Bill Way with the Centurion Way (p105) and Salterns Way (p111). The three routes are linked by a section of the South Coast Cycle Route.

From the railway crossing between Fishbourne Road and Westgate, head along Westgate towards the city centre. Go **SA** at the roundabout and cycle along historic Westgate. Just after Henty Gardens on your left, turn **R** into Mount Lane, following signs for the *Leisure Centre, Station* and *NCR 2*.

Join the cycle path in front of Chichester College. Go **SA** for the South Coast Cycle Route. Join the cycle path in front of Chichester College. Ride past the busy Avenues de Chartres (West) Car Park in front of Westgate Leisure Centre. Continue riding **SA** under the subway for Hunston and the Station. Pass the multi-storey car park and the Smith and Western pub.

After the bridge, turn **R** towards the station car park and the South Coast Cycle Route for Hunston. Ride into the station car park with care and turn **L**, following the blue NCR 2 sign.

Turn **R** onto the very busy road (or push your bike and use the pedestrian crossing nearby). Go across the railway crossing and ride a short distance.

Turn **L** into Canal Wharf, following signs for *SCCR*. Almost immediately, turn **R**, down the track running in front of the Waterside pub. You are now at Chichester Ship Canal.

2Go **L** round the canal. Follow the canal around to the right. Pass Poyntz Bridge and continue **SA**. Stay on the canal path, following the signs for Hunston. This canal path is well-used, wide (for a towpath) and, initially, hard-surfaced. At the end, cross the bridge over the canal.

3Turn **L**, riding on the cycle track that runs alongside the road. At the fence, turn **R** as the track, signed *NCR 2*, veers away from the road.

Follow the path **L**. At the busy road, take care and turn **R**. There's a pavement alongside. At Church Road, turn **R** towards Mundham, following the NCR blue sticker. Turn **R** along Church Mews. At the T-junction, ride **SA** into Church Road.

Ride on until you reach the next T-junction. Turn **R** into Fisher Lane towards South Mundham. Cycle on.

At the triangular junction, take the right fork by riding **SA**, towards Fisher Bramber. Follow this quiet lane through the houses. There's a great 'open' holiday feeling to this area; perhaps it's the sea air washing over the peninsula.

4Cross the cattle grid and continue on the footpath. Sustrans has negotiated its use by non-motorised travellers only, so it's a permissive cycleway.

Do not cross the second cattle grid. At this junction, go **SA** through the gateway, following the NCR 88 sign as you take the path to the **L**.

Ride on this path through the open field. Pass through the gate and ride along the hard or easy-surfaced paths. At the edge of the field, pass over another cattle grid and continue on the concrete bridleway.

At the junction, turn **L** along the track. You are entering Pagham Harbour Area. Ditches have been built here to encourage water voles to take up residence. Turn **R** by Marsh Farm Dairy, following the blue *NCR 88* sign. At the end of the concrete path, at the T-junction, turn **L**, following the blue sign.

At the wooden waymarker, turn **R**, following the *NCR 88* sign to take the (permissive) footpath. Pass by the wooden fence and ride on. This mud track weaves around a couple of fields.

5 At the road, turn **L**. Pass Halsey's Farm as you ride along Mill Lane. Pass The Crab and Lobster pub. Ride **R** at the end of the road and follow it round Pagham Harbour. Pass the benches ideally placed for a picnic on the site of what was once an old mill. After the lone bench, ride **L** on the permissive bridleway, following the wooden waymarker. At the next wooden waymarker, ride **R** again along a permissive bridleway. After a short distance, come to wooden gateposts by the visitor centre for Pagham Nature Reserve.

6 If you wish to continue to Selsey, at present you must venture **L** onto the very busy and fast B2145. An alternative way to reach the coast may be to lock up your bike at the bike racks by the visitor centre and take the footpath through the reserve.

14 ARUNDEL MTB LOOP

Rural bridleways, riverbanks, downland climbs & forest sweeps

TOURIST TRAIL

GRADE: ✳ ✳ ✳ ✳

DISTANCE: 17.5km / 10.9 miles

MAPS: OS Explorer 121

Arundel is a great place for a day out. The combination of Arundel Castle and the River Arun gives the town an atmosphere which is both historic and relaxing and I wanted to explore the surrounding area by bicycle. We've come up with a route, but it's physical and exhilarating rather than leisurely and comfortable. The first stretch of our route is somewhat easier and you could do this as a linear route turning back at Houghton.

The trail wends its way along rural bridleways to roughly follow the course of the River Arun to Houghton. Some bridleways are narrow with stinging nettles so long trousers are advised, there are plenty of gradients and it could be muddy in winter. Having said that, it's fun and the stretch by the river is quite wild and beautiful.

If you decide to do the downland loop, be ready for some serious climbs and some excellent downhills with some great views along the way! You'll certainly deserve a large slice of cake on your return to Arundel.

LINKS WITH
None.

EASY ACCESS
No.

PUBLIC TRANSPORT
TRAIN STATION: Arundel.

TO REACH THE START
SAT NAV MILL ROAD ARUNDEL BN18.
At Arundel, on the A27 Brighton to Chichester road, follow signs to the town centre. Take the first R by the post office into Mill Road.

PARKING
MILL ROAD
There is roadside parking along Mill Road. In high season, you may have to use one of the pay and display car parks.

CASTLE ENTRANCE
Opposite castle entrance. Public WC. Arundel boatyard is inside this car park.

QUEEN STREET
There's also a car park along Queen Street, by Arundel Lido.

HOUGHTON HILL CAR PARK
Offers an out-of-town option, if you don't mind gradients.

BIKE HIRE
M'S CYCLE HIRE
Will deliver bicycles within Arundel, Brighton, Bognor Regis, Chichester, Littlehampton and Worthing, and they can pick up from the same or a different location. They'll also transport luggage / help with information for weekend breaks.
T Maria 07852 986 165 / John 07852 986 163
www.m-cyclehire.co.uk

FOOD, DRINK AND ACCOMMODATION
SWANBOURNE LODGE AND TEA ROOMS
At the entrance to Arundel Park. Hot and cold snacks and meals for refreshment.
T 01903 884 293

THE BLACK RABBIT PUB
Offham, near Arundel. The outstanding feature of this pub is its location. The spacious riverside terrace takes some beating but it can become very busy. Perhaps a good place to rest and watch the world go by after your ride? Food served all day, real ale, play area.
T 01903 882 638
www.theblackrabbitarundel.co.uk

THE GEORGE AND DRAGON, HOUGHTON
Reputedly one of the three oldest pubs in Sussex! Worth cycling to. Offers views over open countryside and freshly prepared food using locally sourced ingredients.
T 01798 831 559
www.thegeorgeanddragonhoughton.co.uk

POINTS OF INTEREST
ARUNDEL PARK
Rowing Boats for hire on Swanbourne Lake. Open all year April – Sept (every day), Oct – March (weekends and school holidays), 10am – 5pm, weather permitting.

ARUNDEL CASTLE
Built at the end of the 11th century, this great castle holds an amazing amount of history within its walls. It's located near the start of our ride.
T 01903 882 173
www.arundelcastle.org

FAMILY RIDING
No.

S Turn **R** to cycle along Mill Road away from Arundel. Pass Arundel Park and Swanbourne Lodge Tea Rooms (with public toilets – 20p charge) on your left. Pass the Wildfowl and Wetlands Trust on your right.

Pass the Black Rabbit pub on your right. Stay on the lane and ride up the short hill. At the T-junction, turn **L** towards South Stoke. Almost immediately, look for the bridleway which is just after the layby.

2 Turn **R** onto the bridleway, passing through the wooden gate. Ride downhill on this narrow winding track. Pass Fox Cottage. Ride beside the bulrushes in the stream/ditch. Go through the gate. Ride on, following the course of the stream. Pass by a wooden fence. Keep riding along this track, with the bulrushes parallel but not right next to you. Follow the track round and up emerging opposite South Stoke Farm.

Turn **L** and then immediately **R** down the public bridleway beside the flint wall. At the end of the flint wall go **L** up the bridleway, following the wooden waymarker. Ride up and then down through some stunning agricultural scenery. Watch out for the bumps!

Go through a gateway and follow the wooden waymarker **R**. Ride (or push) round and up the edge of the field. Go through a gate in the corner of the field, following the wooden bridleway sign **SA** down the hill. There are some HUGE roots on this stretch.

The path levels out. There's a flint wall to the left and if you look carefully through the trees, you can see you are back on course with the River Arun alongside.

Pass a metal kissing gate which leads into Arundel park. Continue cycling along this path.

Ride on along the riverbanks. White 'cliffs' appear out of nowhere, heralded by a flurry of bird alarm calls. Pass a huge oak tree complete with tempting rope swings. Ride on, enjoying the riverbanks. Go through a metal gate and ride straight up, passing a mix of thatched and flint cottages.

3 You are now in Houghton. At the end of South Lane, turn **L** onto the B2139 for a short distance. Pass the George and Dragon. Some may wish to stop here!

To avoid strenuous climbs, retrace your tyre tracks to Arundel along the river side bridleways.

Shortly after the pub and the private road, there's a bridleway. Go **R** along this track which takes you on Monarch's Way. It is a steep track and you might want to push! At the top, go **SA**, heading for the wooden waymarker. Ride **R**.

On the brow of the hill, stop to draw breath and admire the far-reaching view. Look for the bridleway marker which signs you to follow a narrow track between the trees. Ride on. This stretch runs along the ridge and is flatter and easier. After the car park, a steady upward gradient kicks in again. No shame in pushing...

Emerge at a chalky field and follow the bridleway **SA**.

At the road, go across and ride **SA** on the bridleway, ignoring the left fork. Ride a short distance down the slope, looking out for the wooden marker post. Ride **L** on the signed bridleway. At the next post, when you emerge from the trees onto a clear path, head **L** towards the car park. Emerge at Whiteways Café.

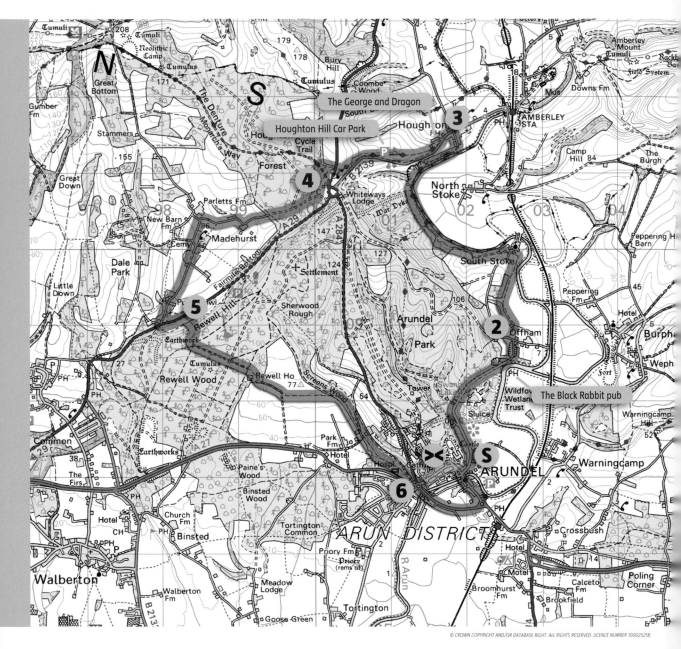

The George and Dragon

Houghton Hill Car Park

The Black Rabbit pub

4 Turn **R** onto the A29 roundabout (!). Take the first **R** on the A29 towards Bognor Regis. Almost immediately, turn **R** towards Madehurst. To avoid this nasty little stretch on the A29, walk your bike across the grass in front of the cafe to meet with the Madehurst road. Enjoy this glorious descent on a smooth road. You should get up enough speed to go up the other side without expending any effort. Pass Lower Farm, Stable House and a letterbox. Ride on.

In Madehurst, ignore the lane on the right. Ride **SA** towards Slindon. Pass New Barn Farm and Madehurst Cricket Club. Ride past Old School House and the church. Enjoy yet another sweeping descent. At the A29, turn **L**. After a short distance, look for a green bridleway sign on your right. (If you reach the layby you've gone too far.)

5 Go **R** on the green-signed bridleway, passing through the gate into Fairmile Bottom Nature Reserve and, yes, I'm afraid it is up a hill. Push or ride straight up and across the field towards the treeline.

Go through the gate and push your bike up the steep, but relatively short slope. If you can ride it, good for you! Even pushing your bike, by the top, you will certainly know where your calf muscles are but you won't care, you'll just be glad to be at the top.

At the bridleway post, go **SA**. At the next bridleway post there is a 'star-like' crossroads. Bear diagonally **L** on the main bridleway, riding into Rewell Wood. Ride through the trees. At the forest road, go **SA** on the bridleway. Keep riding.

When you emerge from the woods, go **L**. Where the track curves, go **SA** on to the bridleway following the wooden waymarker. Pass through a gate and ride on, staying on the bridleway.

Pass through a gate, go diagonally across a field and through another gate. Ride down the track through the trees. Keep riding on this wide, leafy bridleway. It's a great downhill with no pedal power required.

After passing the house on your right, ride **SA** following the track – a brilliant bumpy descent on this last stretch of bridleway.

6 You are now back at Arundel. You have a choice: the easiest route back to the start is via the A27. Follow the A27 across the roundabout, exiting towards Brighton and Littlehampton. Cross the bridge over the Arun and cycle on. At the next roundabout head **L** along Queen Street, over the bridge and **R** back into Mill Road.

✂ OPTIONAL RETURN
Alternatively, at the A27 roundabout, head along Maltravers Road into Arundel town centre to wend your way back to the High Street. This option involves at least one hill but the choice is yours. You'll find Mill Road at the bottom of the High Street.

15 THE DOWNS LINK

CYCLEWAY

DISTANCE: 59km / 37 miles in 6 stages

MAPS: OS Explorers 122, 134, 145. County Council maps available

The Downs Link is an amazing facility that links the North Downs and the South Downs. It effectively connects Guildford (via the River Wey) with the South Coast. It's top end is at St Martha's Hill in the Surrey Hills Area of Outstanding Natural Beauty. The trail is an impressive 59km long and, for most of that distance, leads you through Surrey and Sussex countryside via disused railway lines. There are small 'links' across the odd field or via a road or two but, generally, this trail offers traffic-free, easy riding.

It is not only a great trail for long-distance cyclists but many stretches are ideal for easy cycle rides for families, beginners and those looking for hassle-free routes where they can improve their fitness. Of course, our bodies need food just as much as exercise, so we've included convenient places for you to stop for sustenance. A slab of chocolate cake, a fried breakfast or sandwich and chips tastes extra-satisfying after a good cycle ride.

Cycleways provide an important corridor for wildlife because they enable animals to travel around safely and avoid cars too! They usually make their move when us humans aren't around but while cycling on the Downs Link I have seen rabbits, a stoat, deer, a long-eared owl and a mink. If only the latter had been an otter! These elusive and rare creatures have recently been reintroduced to Sussex so maybe one day we'll spot one at dusk or dawn! Keep your eyes peeled...

The trail is well signposted and directions are usually straightforward. I include a detailed write-up of each section not

continued...

just so that you will know exactly where to go, but also to help you pick out the right section for your ride, and information on accommodation and eating places to help make your trip a success.

I have written up the trail travelling south to north, so the stages are therefore described in reverse order: Stage 6 from Shoreham-by-Sea, to Stage 1 at St Martha's Hill. This way you finish with the off-road climbs up towards St Martha's Hill. As this section is tough, you may decide that you would rather finish with the easier run down towards the seaside!

As the bulk of the route is in West Sussex, I have included it all in this section.

LINKS WITH
NCR 2, also known as the South Coast Cycle Route.

Guildford to Cranleigh stretch of NCR 22.

River Wey Towpath to Guildford.

Leith Hill: Those with lots of energy to burn should leave the Downs Link at Run Common and head east, choosing quiet lanes and bridleways through Winterfold Wood and Hurt Wood to reach Leith Hill.

EASY ACCESS
Path surfaces vary from tarmac to bumpy mud but they mainly seem to be a mix of mud and stone. Tarmac sections are the exception rather than the rule and tend to be short. Some sections have steep gradients and there are often short, steep slopes at access points and road crossings. The length of this cycleway makes it hard to be specific but I have included pointers to short sections which may be of interest.

PUBLIC TRANSPORT
TRAIN STATIONS: Shoreham-by-Sea, Horsham, Shalford, Godalming, Chilworth. BUS: Bus timetables for services stopping in Guildford, Shalford, Cranleigh, Rudgwick, Slinfold, Horsham:
www.arrivabus.co.uk

BUS: Horsham–Henfield–Brighton
www.stagecoachbus.com

BIKE HIRE
SOUTHWATER CYCLES
Easy access onto Downs Link at Southwater. Advance booking strongly recommended.
T 01403 701 002
www.southwatercycles.com

PEDAL AND SPOKE
Popular Peaslake cycle shop has opened a flagship store in Cranleigh.
www.pedalandspoke.co.uk

FOOD AND DRINK, ACCOMMODATION STAGE 6
TIP For more B&B accommodation near the Downs Link, try the Cyclists Welcome website.
www.cyclistswelcome.co.uk

SHOREHAM BEACH
SEASONAL KIOSK
Beside beach at Widewater Lagoon with a couple of tables. Great for a hot drink or basic burgers with the kids.

BEACH CAFE, FERRY ROAD
Free Wi-Fi.
T 01273 452 422

SHOREHAM-BY-SEA
TEDDY'S, 12 EAST STREET
Homemade cakes – and these cakes have to be seen to be believed! Also a wide range of speciality teas, cream teas, breakfasts, sandwiches, and light lunches. Family friendly with a relaxed atmosphere. Can be busy.
T 01273 441 186

BRIGHTON CITY AIRPORT
Usually open 7am to 6pm but check for occasional private functions. See points of interest.
T 01273 452 300
www.flybrighton.com

Various other eating options/pubs in Shoreham-by-Sea.

BRAMBER
CASTLE INN HOTEL
3* inn accommodation and restaurant.
T 01903 812 102
www.castleinnhotel.co.uk

THE OLD TOLLGATE RESTAURANT & HOTEL
Best in summer when cream teas can be taken in the garden. Booking essential for Carvery Restaurant, bar snack area small and windowless. 38 en suite rooms in main building or annexe. Secluded car park, padlocked gated area where bikes can be left overnight. Decent breakfast. Best Western.
T 01903 879 494
www.oldtollgatehotel.com

STAGE 5
STEYNING
NASH MANOR
Participating in Cyclists/Walkers Welcome Scheme and have been awarded the Gold Mark for the Green Tourism Scheme. Reflexology available. Enquire for B&B.
T 01903 814 988
www.nashmanor.co.uk

HENFIELD
Henfield is a small town with some eclectic shops – well worth a browse – and some tempting tea rooms.

THE CAT AND CANARY
Right beside the Downs Link. Large garden, down-to-earth, unpretentious. Sunday carveries and Indian specials. Harveys beer.
T 01273 492 509

STAGE 4
PARTRIDGE GREEN
STAN'S BIKE SHACK
Right on the Downs Link! Small shop area. Hot drinks, snacks, gluten-free cakes. Open 7 days.
T 01403 710 514
www.stansbikeshack.coffee

THE PARTRIDGE
Friendly, relaxed, large garden.
T 01403 710 391
www.darkstarpubs.co.uk/contact

WEST GRINSTEAD
THE ORCHARD FAMILY RESTAURANT
With large garden. Extensive menu, good value. Breakfasts, snacks, meals. Open 7 days a week.
T 01403 865 693
www.theorchardrestaurant.moonfruit.com

MAPLEHURST
THE WHITE HORSE
Traditional pub, free house: definitely worth investigating! Lunch is served between 12pm and 2pm (2.30pm on Sundays).
T 01403 891 208
www.whitehorsemaplehurst.co.uk

STAGE 3
SOUTHWATER
SOUTHWATER COUNTRY PARK CAFE
Large terrace overlooking lake. Snacks and light meals. Good spot for a picnic too. WCs.
T 01403 215 256

Various eating options nearby including cafes, pubs and takeaways.

NR SOUTHWATER
THE BAX CASTLE AT TWO MILE ASH
Traditional Sussex pub. Real ale free house. Large open fire in the winter. Home-cooked food and large garden with children's play area. Cycle railings where you can lock your bike.
T 01403 730 369
www.baxcastle.co.uk

SLINFOLD
THE RED LYON
Home-cooked food in this 17th century pub with garden and four well-equipped guest rooms.
T 01403 790 339
www.theredlyon.co.uk

RUDGWICK
THE KING'S HEAD, CHURCH STREET
Turn **L** past the Co-op and ride **SA** at the small roundabout. The pub's on your right at the TOP of a LONG HILL but it is recommended by the locals. Italian gastropub serving a mix of Italian and English food, such as lasagne, gammon, egg & chips.
T 01403 822 200
www.kingsheadrudgwick.co.uk

THE MILK CHURN
Just north of Rudgwick and adjacent to the Downs Link. Follow the milk churns along Lynwick Street. This cafe is on the Bookham Harrison Farm, producers of the famed Sussex Charmer and Twineham Grange cheese. If you haven't tasted it yet, you should! Open 7 days.
T 01403 823 980
http://milkchurn.co.uk

STAGE 2
CRANLEIGH

Cycle racks outside Sainsbury's or in town centre. Cranleigh Leisure Centre, pool & cafe, toilets. Open-air fitness station. A wide mix of places to eat including:

CROMWELL COFFEE HOUSE
Good value, fresh food, sunny terrace.
T 01483 273 783

SHAMLEY GREEN
THE RED LION INN
T 01483 892 202
www.redlionshamleygreen.com

STAGE 1
BRAMLEY

Bramley village is in a conservation area. Explore the High Street with its various shops and eating establishments.

THE JOLLY FARMER
Six en suite rooms and a flat available.
T 01483 893 355
www.jollyfarmer.co.uk

THE WHEATSHEAF
T 01483 892 722
www.wheatsheaf-bramley.co.uk

THE BRAMLEY CAFE
Good value, fully licensed cafe.
www.bramleycafe.com

SHALFORD (ALSO IN RIVER WEY TOWPATH GUIDE)
THE PARROT INN
Family-owned and family-run. Large terrace where you can keep your bikes safe. Children welcome at lunch and up to 8pm. Six en suite rooms.
T 01483 561 400
www.parrotinn.co.uk

BLACKHEATH
THE VILLAGERS INN, BLACKHEATH LANE
Large garden. Home-cooked food and seafood. Chalet rooms available.
T 01483 893 152
www.thevillagersinn.co.uk

POINTS OF INTEREST
STAGE 6
BRIGHTON CITY AIRPORT
More atmospheric than most. It's a working airport for light aircraft with emergency services stationed here. The main building is art deco and has been used as a setting for several television programmes including Tenko and Poirot and, more recently, films such as The Woman In Gold and The Da Vinci Code. There's a visitor centre, airport tours, and a restaurant/bar.
www.flybrighton.com

STAGE 5
BRAMBER CASTLE
You may picnic in the grounds of this English Heritage Norman motte and bailey castle (admission free). There's space for children to run around. Built around 1070, the most prominent feature today is the ruined Gatehouse Tower. The children of William de Braose, starved to death by King John, are said to return and haunt the castle and 15th Century Lady Maud wanders unhappily. She was found dead after she discovered her husband bricking up the dungeon that imprisoned her lover. No facilities but toilets at nearby parking. No admission charge.
www.english-heritage.org.uk

STAGE 3
SOUTHWATER COUNTRY PARK
The Visitor Centre, which offers information, toilets and a cafe, with outside terrace, is open every weekend and most days during the school holidays. There are three lakes: Cripplegate, the base for Southwater Watersports Centre; Lennoxwood, a day ticket fishery; and Quarry, a haven for wildlife. Naturally, the other two lakes are popular with wildlife too. Whether you want to join in the activity or just soak up the atmosphere, there's always plenty going on. Good place for a picnic. Play area. Family 'beach' area where water is sectioned off for swimming.

STAGE 2
RUDGWICK
Fossils of a unique new dinosaur were found in the brickworks. It was named after the village: Polacanthus Rudgwickensis.

BAYNARDS TUNNEL

Was the highest point of the Guildford-Horsham branch line at 250 feet above sea level. It was also the scene of the only loss of life during the construction of this railway line. On the night of 27th August 1863, one of the line inspectors was killed in Baynards Tunnel. The London, Brighton and South Coast Railway company (LBSCR) paid his funeral expenses of £10, and gave a donation of £13.13s to his widow.

STAGE 1

WEY & ARUN CANAL

Boat trips along the Wey and Arun Canal, provided by the Canal Trust, who aim to restore the canal – which runs through Surrey and West Sussex – back to navigation. *www.weyandarun.co.uk*

ST MARTHA'S HILL

St Martha's Hill is 160m (525ft) above sea level. On a clear day you can see eight counties from the top. Part of the hill is Colyers Hanger Site of Special Scientific Interest, managed by Surrey Wildlife Trust. Erosion is a problem with this site so please keep to the bridleways. St Martha's Church on the Hill is a listed building and a well-loved landmark. It was rebuilt in 1850 and is on the site of a Saxon church.

FAMILY RIDING

Some stretches are brilliant for families, others less so. Check comments under individual sections.

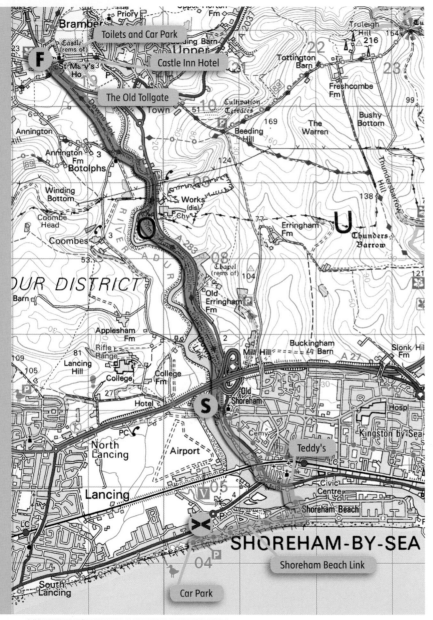

Map labels:
- Toilets and Car Park
- Castle Inn Hotel
- The Old Tollgate
- Teddy's
- Shoreham Beach Link
- Car Park

STAGE 6

GRADE *

DISTANCE

Shoreham-by-Sea – Botolphs – Bramber
6.6km / 4.1 miles

Shoreham Beach to Downs Link at
Shoreham-by-Sea 3.5km / 2.2 miles

EASY ACCESS

Wide, mud path starts at Shoreham. It can
be bumpy and does become narrow and less
even around the old cement works.

PARKING

WIDEWATER LAGOON, SHOREHAM BEACH
Height barrier, fee payable in high season.
Right beside Shoreham seafront cycle path
but also handy for the Downs Link.

RIVERSIDE CAR PARK (LONG STAY),
SHOREHAM BEACH
Is even closer, beside the footbridge.

FAMILY RIDING

Off-road, flat path although can be muddy.
Park at Bramber to avoid pushing/road on
the link from Shoreham Beach.

STAGE 6
SHOREHAM-BY-SEA – BOTOLPHS – BRAMBER

The Downs Link starts as a mud path. It's a good surface in most weather conditions and its decent width means you can easily skirt round puddles if you prefer. About 1 ½ miles from Shoreham, pass a layby. Follow the mud track round the back of the old cement works. The grounds appear to be being used by various transport companies and the place feels less desolate than in previous years. Ride alongside the River Adur.

Arrive at Botolphs by the bridge. Botolphs is the meeting point of the South Downs Way and the Downs Link. You can go east to Devils Dyke or west to Washington. Alternatively, head for the North Downs Way via the Downs Link – a mere 34 ½ miles away! The name of the Downs Link cycleway is well-deserved!

Turn **L** across the bridge, following the Downs Link towards the North Downs Way. Ride **L** away from the river, following the wooden waymarker **L**. At the corner with the bench, go **R** to stay on the Downs Link (**L** to follow the South Downs Way). Follow the wooden sign as the path goes to the right and then the left in a 'S' bend towards the road.

Emerge at the road and **cross with care**, following the green Downs Link sign, to cycle **L** on the track.

Arrive in Bramber at the busy roundabout. Go **R** to find the pubs, over the road and **L** up the steep driveway to explore Bramber Castle, or **SA**, following the Downs Link sign along the minor road, to keep cycling north towards Henfield.

LINK FROM SHOREHAM BEACH TO DOWNS LINK AT SHOREHAM-BY-SEA

The best parking is at Shoreham Beach but the link is currently by road. Families could park at Riverside and push until Rope Tackle. This link should alter as planned improvements are made to paths and the footbridge, thanks to the far-thinking Sustrans Connect2 scheme to create networks for everyday journeys, so do keep a close eye on the signs.

From Widewater Lagoon, ride **SA** on the road, following the NCR 2 blue signs. At the T-junction, turn **R**, following the NCR sign. As King's Walk curves, leave the road to go **SA**, riding parallel with the beach huts. Ride past the gate, still following the NCR signs **SA** as you cycle past an eclectic mix of seventies 'beach' houses.

Turn **L** down Ferry Road, passing the Beach Café on your right. Turn **L** into Riverside. Head **R**, either through the car park or the concrete bollards a bit further on, and **push your bike across the footbridge**.

Head **L** along the High Street passing the Rope Tackle Apartments. Turn **L** down Rope Tackle Road. Follow the road round and turn **L** into Broad Reach, just before the train line. See the River Adur estuary ahead and turn **R** to take the riverbank path under the railway bridge. Follow the muddy, rough path towards a distant Lancing College.

The path becomes tarmac. Pass picnic tables which have a good view of light aircraft taking off and landing at Shoreham Airport. There's an entrance from the road on your right. At the Millenium Bridge, go **L** for Shoreham Airport or **SA** for the Downs Link.

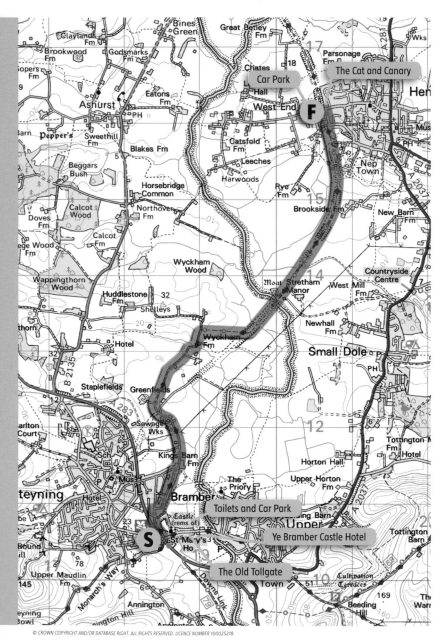

STAGE 5

GRADE ✱ ✱

DISTANCE
Bramber – Steyning – Henfield
7.7km / 4.8 miles

EASY ACCESS
Not great. The road surfaces soon become very rough leading out of Bramber. Hilly and pot-holed! The mud and stone bridleway section leading south from Henfield to the old railway bridges and the River Adur could be accessible in good conditions. Path could be muddy as bridleway is well used. Steep-ish slope at the path start point.

PARKING
BRAMBER
The Street car park, opposite Ye Bramber Castle Hotel. Free, and with toilets.

Also parking at Bramber Castle.

To reach Downs Link from The Street car park, go **R** up the hill to the roundabout.

FAMILY RIDING
A great introduction to bumpy surfaces and hills for older kids. All off-road or very quiet roads. Younger families should stick to the shorter mud and stone bridleway section leading south from Henfield to the old railway bridges and the River Adur.

STAGE 5

BRAMBER – STEYNING – HENFIELD

At the roundabout, go **R** following the small Downs Link sign **SA** along the road, which is signed unsuitable for heavy vehicles. At the end of Castle Lane, go **SA** into Roman Road, following the green Downs Link sign.

Take the first **R** into King's Stone Avenue. Ride to the very end of the road. Turn **R**, following the green Downs Link sign. Follow the lane as it curves to the left along King's Barn Lane. The lane becomes more rural, climbing as it leads away from Steyning and Bramber. The smell of the water treatment works may keep you pedalling fast!

This tarmac road has occasional cars. Cross the narrow bridge. Keep riding **SA**. There are soon views over the Downs to your right. The surface becomes rough and very uneven. This is definitely a rural road!

Pass a house on your right. At the waymarker, ride by Wyckham Dale Farm, heading **SA**. Enjoy the ups and downs of a bumpy pothole-strewn downhill before curving through the farm to take the sharp climb back up the rutted hill with some serious pedal-power. The views at the top are worth the effort.

Take a **R** at the wooden waymarker by the metal gate. Sweep down the next slightly more level stretch of path.

Cross the old railway bridge. The path surface here is firm, more level and generally easier to cycle. Pass another two railway bridges. The second crosses the River Adur. Notice the bridleway just before the bridge: this is where the Henfield route in *Cycling in Sussex (ISBN: 978 1 906148 07 2, Vertebrate Publishing 2008)* leads off across agricultural bridleways and hidden lanes.

Cross a brick bridge. The surface now is a mix of compacted stone, shingle and mud. You are riding along the top of an old embankment as you come into the outskirts of Henfield.

Cross a farm lane. Ride on following a wooden waymarker.

At the end of this Downs Link section, there's a very short road link. Follow the green Downs Link sign **R**, then do the swift climb up Lower Station Road. At the top, go **L** where you will see the Downs Link car park beside the pub or **R** along Station Road to explore Henfield.

STAGE 4

GRADE ✳

DISTANCE
Henfield – Partridge Green – West Grinstead – Southwater 11.4km / 7.1 miles

EASY ACCESS
West Grinstead Station has easy parking and an easy-surfaced trail heading in both directions. Another good option would be to join the trail from the public footpath opposite the Partridge pub at Partridge Green. You soon turn **R** to join the Downs Link. You then have a very nice, long, firm-surfaced and easy stretch of old railway line which takes you through West Grinstead Station right to Southwater Country Park.

PARKING
HENFIELD
The A281 runs through Henfield. Near the traffic lights at the pedestrian crossing on the High Street, follow the brown sign for the leisure centre and turn off westwards into Church Street. Continue into Upper Station Road. Park next to the Downs Link, just beyond the Cat and Canary pub.

WEST GRINSTEAD STATION
Car park off the A272. Look out for The Orchard Family Restaurant.

COPSALE
Leave the A24 to take the lane towards Copsale.

FAMILY RIDING
Excellent.

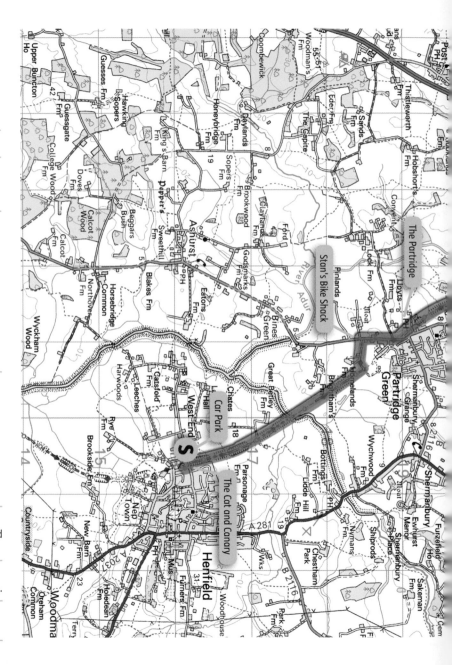

STAGE 4

HENFIELD – PARTRIDGE GREEN – WEST GRINSTEAD – SOUTHWATER

From the Henfield car park, go through the gate and down a short but moderately steep slope to the hard, stony-surfaced Downs Link path. This path runs along the base of an old cutting and is level. There are some beautiful views across the fields. Cross an old railway bridge known as Betley Bridge and go through the gate.

Follow the narrow mud track running **SA** across the grassy field. The River Adur wends its way across the field too. This section could be muddy if wet!

After the field, go through the gate and ride along the bridleway. This path is rough-surfaced, dusty with stones, but generally even and wide. Ignore the footpath to the left.

At the green sign, turn **L** along the Downs Link Bridleway. At the B2135, turn **R** onto the road. There is a grass verge/pavement running alongside this short road link which children could use.

Ignore the first public bridleway. Reach the bridge and go **L** by the Downs Link / Public Bridleway sign. There's a slight slope down to a narrow-ish path. Soon the Downs Link crosses a lane. Turn **R** and **walk along the footpath** for the Partridge pub or ride **SA** to stay on the Downs Link.

This section of the Downs Link is lined by trees with a wide, easy-riding track. Before you know it, you'll ride over a metal bridge, go through a tunnel and arrive at old West Grinstead Station.

West Grinstead Station has its own car park and picnic tables. Kids will love the old railway carriage and platform. There's even a signal! The Orchard Family Restaurant makes a good pit stop too!

Ride on. The path remains easy riding, running along the top of an old embankment with views through the trees and across fields.

Reach Copsale car park. This is where the Bridge House pub is but it's currently not open. If you're looking for a pub, try leaving the Downs Link and cycling **R** towards Maplehurst where you will find the White Horse pub.

Cross the lane and ride **SA** up the short slope following the Downs Link signs. Ride on another nice easy stretch of track. Come to the water treatment works.

Go **L** through the bridge under the A24. Ride to the end of Stakers Lane. This lane is wide and tarmac but slightly uneven. Cross the road and cycle **SA** to continue on the Downs Link.

Ride **L** to enjoy the facilities at Southwater Country Park.

STAGE 3

GRADE ✳ / ✳ ✳

DISTANCE
Southwater – Christ's Hospital – Slinfold –
Rudgwick 12km / 7.5 miles

EASY ACCESS
Southwater Country Park has easy access paths.
South from the old station from Rudgwick
to Slinfold the Downs Link follows a section
of old railway line and is probably accessible
in good conditions. Slopes at road crossings.

PARKING
SOUTHWATER COUNTRY PARK
Turn into Cripplegate Lane from the main
A24. Pass Southwater Country Park entrance
and turn **L** into Station Road Car Park.

FAMILY RIDING
The stretch between Christ's Hospital
and Slinfold is only suitable for families
comfortable with trickier road cycling.

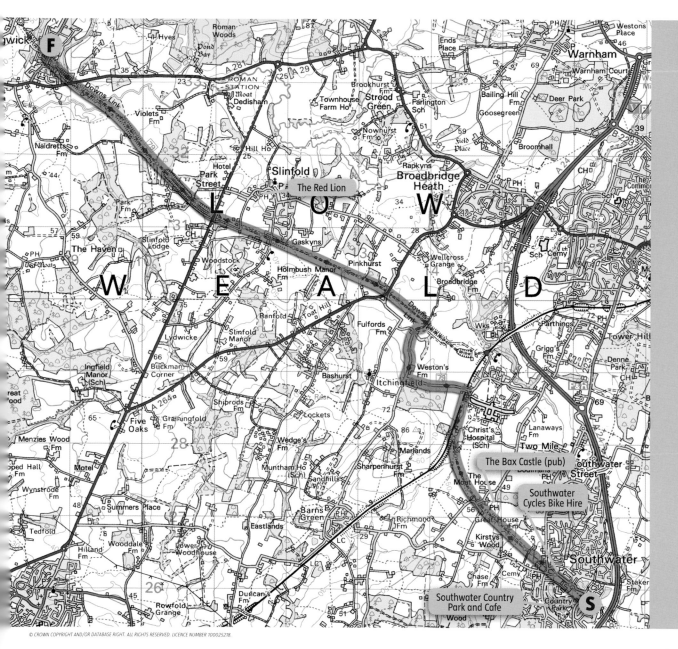

The Red Lion

The Bax Castle (pub)

Southwater Cycles Bike Hire

Southwater Country Park and Cafe

STAGE 3

SOUTHWATER – CHRIST'S HOSPITAL – SLINFOLD – RUDGWICK

The Downs Link runs between the car park and Southwater Country Park. To ride north towards Rudgwick, turn **R** out of the car park. Ride along a path with houses either side. Come into Southwater. Use the pedestrian crossing to cross the busy road. The bike hire and coffee shops are off to the right.

To stay on the Downs Link, ride on between the wooden fences. Pass through the tunnel and along the path between the fences. Go through the gate and **SA** across the field. Pass through a second gate and continue on the track **SA**, following the green Downs Link signs. Continue along this gravel and mud path. If you're thirsty or hungry, look out for access to Bax Castle pub!

Go under the bridge and ride onward on this level, wooded path. Emerge at the boundary of Christ's Hospital. Go through the gap and continue in the same direction, following the Downs Link signs. Keep **SA** at the wooden waymarker.

Turn **L** at the road, following the Downs Link sign, and then **L** again. Ride over the bridge and along the country road. Turn **R** at the T-junction.

Watch out for the farm. Just after this, **there's a downward run and a rather busy stretch of road: it's not ideal for young children**.

Take care as you reach the curve. You may want to dismount. It's a dangerous bend where you need to turn **R**, following the green Downs Link signs.

Ride up the slope, over the bridge and at the green sign, double back on yourself through the gate on the **L**. Go **R** beside the tunnel. Pass the airstrip and ride on. Go through a gate, cross the road, through another gate. Cycle on.

Go through the gate. You are at Slinfold. Detour into the village if you wish to pop into the pub.

Otherwise ride on. Don't miss the double bridge over the River Arun. This is the fine example of Victorian engineering that inspired the Downs Link signpost. As you approach it, there's a path on your right to a viewing spot / small glade on the riverbanks where you could stop for a rest.

After the metal gate, cross the road and continue **SA** following the green Downs Link sign. You will arrive at the site of the old railway station at Rudgwick.

STAGE 2

GRADE ✳ ✳

DISTANCE
Rudgwick – Baynards – Cranleigh –
Run Common 10.8km / 6.7 miles

EASY ACCESS
North of Rudgwick is very hilly. At old Baynards
station, there's a short stretch of easy path
to the picnic area. The path by Cranleigh
Leisure Centre is concrete. Heading north from
Cranleigh Leisure Centre, there is a short sharp
incline at the access point to the hard surfaced
track by the road.

PARKING
Cranleigh Leisure Centre.

FAMILY RIDING
There are some significant gradients on the
woodland paths around Baynards Tunnel.

POINTS OF INTEREST
Shortly after Rudgwick, this stage crosses
from Sussex into Surrey.

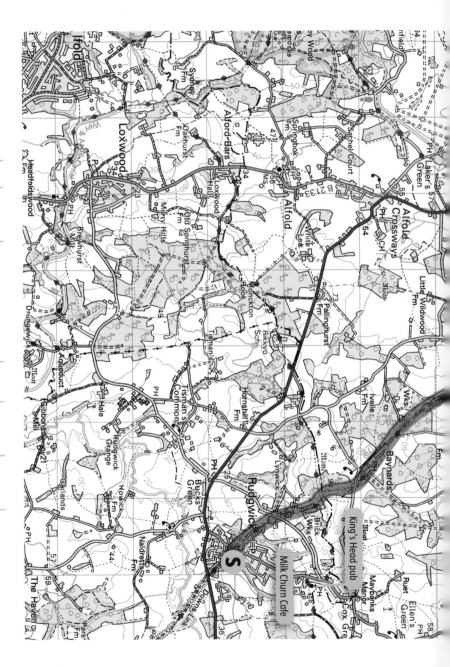

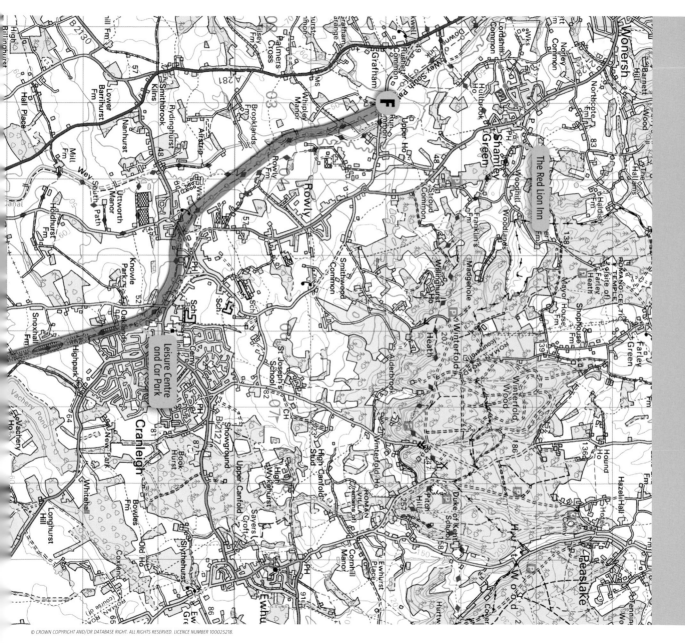

STAGE 2

RUDGWICK – BAYNARDS – CRANLEIGH – RUN COMMON

Cycle towards Cranleigh on the mud track which leads you through the woods. As you climb up the steep slope (you can't miss it!), look right to see closed-up Baynards Tunnel. Keep climbing. Pass the well-placed bench and ride **SA** through beautiful broadleaf South Wood.

You are on the Sussex Border Path as well as the Downs Link for a very short stretch. At the wooden waymarker, cycle **R**. **Cross into Surrey** and enjoy the downhill sweep through the woodland. I guess that's the advantage of long-distance cycling – you know you're not going back up the hill anytime soon.

Reach the road by the brick bridge. Knowing where to go isn't obvious here unless you've already done it because there are two possibilities:

Walkers may go **R**, following the wooden Downs Link sign. Just after the brick bridge, turn **R** through the wooden markers and then sharp **R** to follow the track under the bridge and along the path of the old railway. Emerge at the wooden gate. Go **L** and then **R** in front of the old station.

Cyclists should go **L** along Baynards Lane but, very soon, after the walled house but before the red phone box, turn **R**. At the phone box, go **R** to stay on the Downs Link. (If you take the wooden-signed bridleway to go **SA**, it will link up with the Downs Link after the woodland section.) Ride **R** between the walls, past the now closed Thurlow Arms, and you will soon come to Baynards Station. Pick up the Downs Link sign in front of the old station and turn **L** here.

Baynards Station is now a privately owned residence. From the station, go through the wooden gate. Pass through a picnic area with several tables and continue along this easy and pleasant wooded track. By the pond, on your left, keep cycling **SA** round the gate.

Emerge on a track by some playing fields in Cranleigh. There's a large play area with picnic tables on your right. As you pass Cranleigh Leisure Centre, you may be tempted to stop and play with the open-air workout station which includes a sealed chest press, an air skier and a rowing machine.

In front of the workstation, take the **R** fork and leave the concrete path to follow the shingle track. Cross the bridge and ride through the wooden posts.

The path emerges at the back of Marks & Spencer.

Head **R** to sample the delights of Cranleigh, a small but bustling town with an open feel to it.

Head **L** on the mud track to cross the road. Go **SA** on the wooden waymarked Downs Link, following the hard-surfaced track **R** and then **L**.

Ride on. This easy-surfaced path runs through Cranleigh. Eventually, the track turns to mud and passes under an old railway tunnel. Keep pedalling. In winter, you may see some puddles on this stretch.

Ride **SA** on the stone bridge. Views open out on your right to distant tree-covered hills. Climb the slope. The path levels out. The track is a mixture of mud and stone. Ride on.

STAGE 1

LINKS WITH
See p179 for the River Wey Towpath which links with this stage.

GRADE ✳ ✳ ✳ ✳

DISTANCE
Run Common – Bramley – St Martha's Hill
10.5km / 6.5 miles

EASY ACCESS
From old Bramley and Wonersh Station to the towpath should be accessible in good conditions. The car park includes a wheelchair-accessible ramp down to the path.

PARKING
From Guildford or Horsham, take the A281 to the turn-off between Grafham and Birtley Green to Rowley and Cranleigh. After 1.2 km park in the layby just after the bridge over the Downs Link.

STATION ROAD OFF THE HIGH STREET, BRAMLEY
Car park at Station Road off the High Street, Bramley at site of the old station.

WONERSH COMMON ROAD
Car park off Wonersh Common Road.

CHURCH OF ST MARTHA'S ON THE HILL
Car park for Church of St Martha's on the Hill, off Guildford Lane.

To reach the Downs Link from St Martha's Hill car park head over the small wooden bridge to the left of the noticeboard and follow the mud track **R** as it zig-zags up the hill. After the World War 2 pill box, look for the wooden waymarker pointing left.

FAMILY RIDING
This stretch is good for families but at Tannery Lane Bridge switch to the towpath for an easy ride. Blackheath Common is beautiful so brave the sandy climb up there if you wish. The climb up St Martha's Hill is very hard going, even for adults.

STAGE 1
RUN COMMON – BRAMLEY – ST MARTHA'S HILL

This stretch of the Downs Link leads you through the green fields of Surrey. This mud and stone stretch of path runs along the top of an old embankment and should be good for families. You are climbing but it's very gradual.

The trail shares the Wey South Path but you won't see the Wey & Arun Canal here. It was in operation from 1816 to 1868 when traffic moved from canal to rail to road. You can't see it here now.

Shortly after a wooden footbridge, notice the wooden waymarker signed *R22*. Go **L** for the Shamley Green NCR 22 Link. Go **SA** for the Downs Link, NCR 22.

The path turns to conglomerate / concrete as it comes into Bramley, on a slight uphill.

Emerge at the old Bramley and Wonersh station. A railway crossing marks the road but you must make your own way across. Go **L** along Station Road to reach the High Street. It offers a selection of pubs.

There's a covered bus shelter on the old platform with benches if you fancy an undercover picnic.

Follow the track. Soon the path again passes near to the site of the old Wey & Arun Canal and although there are no benches, there is space to picnic in the trees by what presumably used to be the canal bank.

Ride on to Tannery Lane Bridge, a 'turnover' or 'roving' bridge where the towpath changes sides.

At this bridge, you could continue **SA** on the River Wey towpath. See p179 for more information on this trail, which takes you right into Guildford. For families and those who prefer easy riding this would be your best bet.

Alternatively, if you want to follow the Downs Link to the start, head **R** across the bridge.

The next section of the Downs Link is on uneven off-road bridleways of mud and sand with a significant amount of climbing involved.

After the bridge, go **L**. At the road, turn **R**. Pass Droges Close.

Soon, at the top of Tannery Lane, cross the road and follow the wooden Downs Link sign **SA** onto the mud bridleway. The soil is very sandy now and can be hard-going, especially when wet.

At the top of a steep but short-ish climb, the path turns **R** (ignore the stile to the footpath). Enjoy a muddy downhill.

At the junction, follow the bridleway **L**. The footpath leads **R** up to Chinthurst Hill Nature Reserve and Tower. Follow the track **SA** past the Downs Link noticeboard, passing the Wonersh Common Road car park.

The bridleway emerges by a wooden waymarker at the road. Cross the road diagonally to your **R** and follow the track into the woods. Ride past Great Tangley manor, where the path curves towards Upper Tangley Manor. Follow the wooden waymarked Downs Link **SA**.

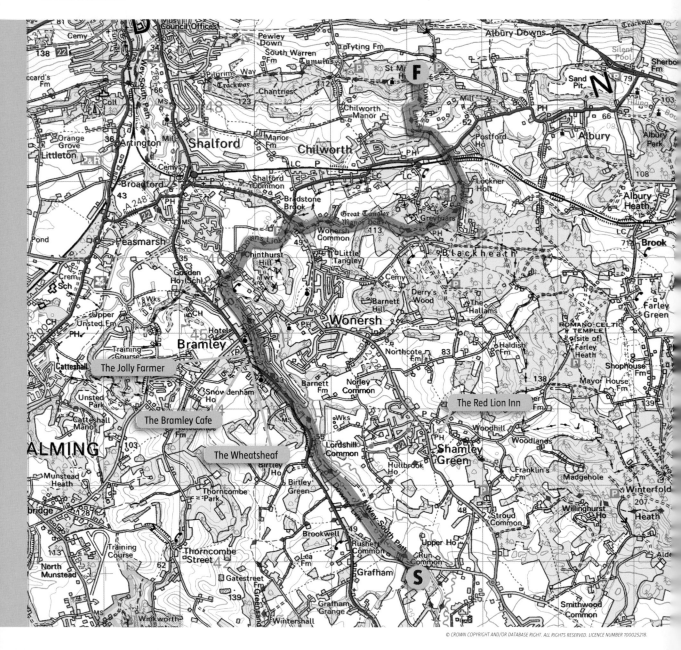

Once more, the soil becomes very sandy on this narrow, uphill bridleway. It's steep so you will have to see if you can cycle all the way up: you may prefer to push. It's bordered by private woodland. The paths level out at the top and you are rewarded with views to the hills beyond the valleys. Ride on.

At the crossroads, follow the Downs Link **SA**. Where the path becomes more hard-surfaced and joins the driveway, continue riding **SA** down the hill.

Reach a road. Cross it and follow the bridleway **SA**. See the sign for Blackheath on your right. Almost immediately, turn **R** onto a track, following the wooden waymarker.

This uphill track is very sandy. It takes some effort but it's beautiful: flanked by pine woodland on one side, and Blackheath Common on the other, as it climbs steeply upwards.

At the top, take time to wander over to the war memorial. They've chosen a stunning spot to build it and the views and ambience are quite something.

If you want to continue on to St Martha's Hill ride **SA** on the Downs Link, looking out for the occasional white circles and blue marker posts. This next section requires significant climbing on off-road bridleways. Some of these tracks have uneven or deep muddy surfaces which can become churned up, especially when wet.

Cross the small private road and follow the wooden waymarked Downs Link **SA**. The path is soon split by a fence with the bridleway on the right and the footpath on the left. The track narrows as it goes downhill. This stretch is bumpy with some large roots and there's barbed wire that's too close for comfort.

The track emerges at a road. Cross the bridge **SA** and follow the Downs Link wooden signs. At the end of Dorking Road, cross the busier road to ride **SA**. Cross a small bridge. **Dismount** to follow the footpath **L** as it leads you around the remains of Chilworth Gunpowder Mills. Keep pedalling up the hill.

Turn **R** at the wooden waymarker, heading towards the distant church. Ride or push your way up this narrow-ish mud bridleway, following the track right at the wooden waymarker by the metal gate. Follow the path upwards through the woods enjoying some far-reaching views. Towards the top, just before a WW2 pill box, reach a wooden waymarker, a milestone marked *Downs Link* and a noticeboard that's been kicked out at the top of the hill. This is the start of the Downs Link!

There are a number of paths here and they're not all marked. Go **L** on the footpath to climb higher up St Martha's Hill and visit the listed church.

If you want the car park and road, go **R** at the Downs Link marker post, passing the WW2 pill box. Head down the hill.

surrey
& london parks

surrey & london parks

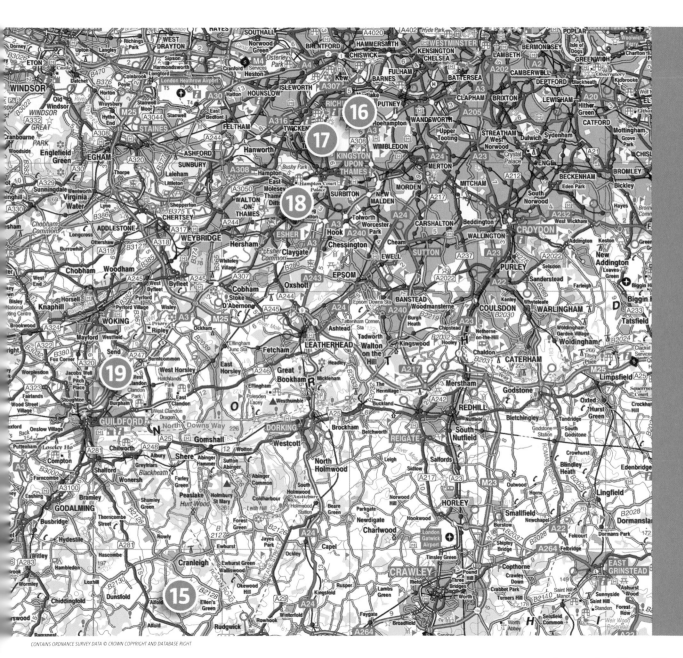

16 THE TAMSIN TRAIL
Richmond Park

COUNTRY PARK

GRADE: ✳ / ✳ ✳

DISTANCE: 12km / 7.5 miles

MAPS: OS Explorer 161; Richmond Park Map

The Tamsin Trail is a 12km long circuit, which runs around the perimeter of historic Richmond Park. This is a shared path with pedestrian priority and there is a 10mph speed limit. As the largest of the royal parks, Richmond Deer Park offers the space and tranquility to escape urban life. Trail viewpoints offer glimpses of London features such as St Paul's Cathedral and the Post Office Tower.

You know you're still in central London but somehow the atmosphere lightens. I don't know whether it's the ancient trees, the grazing deer or the friendly atmosphere as local cyclists congregate, but this trail offers the chance to experience a completely different side of London.

LINKS WITH
NCR 4 Thames Cycle Route.

EASY ACCESS
See *www.royalparks.org.uk* for detailed
disabled access information with
www.disabledgo.com link. Surfaces tend
to be sandy gravel with some gradients.

PUBLIC TRANSPORT
TRAIN STATION: Richmond Station.
Turn **R** just before the bridge to ride to
Richmond Station.

PARKING
There are car parks at several of the gates.
We've chosen to start the circuit at the
Roehampton Gate because this is where
the bike hire is located.

BIKE HIRE
RICHMOND PARK CYCLE HIRE
Open every day in high season.
In partnership with the Royal Parks.
T 07968 697 541 (Opening hours only)
www.parkcycle.co.uk

BLAZING SADDLES BIKE HIRE
At Richmond Bridge boathouses.
T 0208 948 8240
www.blazingsaddlesbikehire.com

BICYCLE
A local independent bike shop in Richmond,
near The Alberts.
T 0208 940 2274
www.bicyclerichmond.co.uk

FOOD AND DRINK
There are four main places to buy food and
drink in Richmond Park:

ROEHAMPTON CAFE
By Roehampton Gate
T 0208 876 7933

PEMBROKE LODGE
Elegant Georgian tea rooms.
T 0208 940 8207

And the refreshment points at Broomfield Hill
and Pen Pond car parks.
T 0207 581 1188

THE ROEBUCK
If you leave Richmond Park via Richmond
Gate and go straight across you will see
The Roebuck on your right. This pub has
a superb location and, during the summer,
you can take your drink across the road to
soak up the views from the top of Richmond
Hill. This pub was a favourite haunt of the
Rolling Stones and dates back to 1500.
T 0208 948 2329
*http://www.taylor-walker.co.uk/pub/
roebuck-richmond/s5628*

POINTS OF INTEREST
RICHMOND PARK
Richmond is famous for its 300 red deer and
350 fallow deer, but centuries of protection
have produced a number of unique and
varied habitats in the 2,500 acres of parkland.
Certain areas of grass and woodland have
enabled some rare invertebrates, flora and
fauna to flourish. Look out for fungi growing
on some of the ancient trees and fallen trunks.
Richmond Park provides such a valuable
environment that it is now a designated
National Nature Reserve and a Site of Special
Scientific Interest. **Consequently, off-road
cycling is not permitted.**
The Park is open from 7am in the summer
and 7.30am in the winter, and closes at dusk
all year round.
www.royalparks.org.uk/parks/richmond_park

FAMILY RIDING
All off-road on easy-riding surfaces but
with some gradients. Watch out for the
road crossings in the park. Deer are an
added attraction.

We've chosen to follow the trail anti-clockwise as this avoids what somebody described to me as 'the mountain' and means you finish with a nice 'n' easy downhill section.

S Leave the car park and go **R** on the shared sandy path. Take care crossing at the small roundabout. Continue **SA** onto the sandy gravel path. Cross a small wooden bridge. You do need to keep a look out for pedestrians and, depending on time and season, some sections of the path may be busier than others. Pass the pond on your left. Cross a small road at Sheen Gate.

Cross the lane and small bridge. Ride on, savouring the beautiful view of trees stretching as far as the eye can see with deer grazing in the foreground if you're lucky. Pedal the slight uphill which takes you to the far side of the park. You will find you're cycling near the walls and fences of the perimeter but there's not a house in sight. The track undulates. Pass another pond on your left.

2 Cross Richmond Gate.

OPTIONAL DIVERSION TO THE ROEBUCK
Follow the road out of Richmond Gate, heading **SA** onto Richmond Hill.

The path may now empty of pedestrians as some follow the footpath leading off to the right. The shared-use path now runs parallel to the road. At the gate to Pembroke Lodge Gardens/ Poet's Corner, take a rest on the Ian Dury Bench to admire views over Twickenham towards Heathrow. The Thames is down there somewhere! Riding is easier on the next section, thanks to the downhill gradient.

3 Pass Pembroke Lodge where there's an information centre, refreshment kiosk, toilets and bike racks.

Enjoy the feeling of space on the next downhill stretch. Cross Ham Gate with care. Here cyclists have a choice: you may turn **L** to follow the red trail through the centre of the park (see Richmond and Thames route! p167) but the Tamsin Trail continues **SA**. This section of the path is narrow tarmac – watch out for the occasional pedestrian as the path swoops up and down with moderate gradients. It's easy to get some speed up, and good for fitness training too.

Cross the road at Kingston Gate and ride over the small wooden bridge. There's a small wooden play area to your left. Keep cycling: the trail runs beside a wall and you can see the house roofs.

4 Pass a pedestrian gate and Broomfield Hill Car park and refreshments. As you cycle on, don't miss the 'City skyscape' views from the hilltop. Is that the Post Office Tower standing sentinel to the left of the 3rd tower block?

You are advised to **dismount** to descend this steep hill. If you don't, watch out for pedestrians and joggers! This quiet stretch is littered with old trees and beefsteak fungus.

Cross the Robin Hood Gate road. By the huge ancient fallen tree trunk, keep **L**, heading back towards Roehampton Gate. Cross the bridge over the stream. Pass the entrance to Richmond Park Golf Course on your right before arriving back at the car park.

17 A LOOP THROUGH RICHMOND DEER PARK
past Ham House & along the Thames

CYCLEWAY	COUNTRY PARK	TOURIST TRAIL
GRADE: ✳		
DISTANCE: 18.5km / 11.5 miles		
MAPS: OS Explorer 161; Richmond Park Map		

This loop is ideal for day-trippers and tourists who would like the chance to explore one of London's most exclusive boroughs on two wheels. In fact, this loop combines the best of both worlds: London buzz and park tranquility. We cut through the centre of peaceful Richmond Park, passing the deer pen. The route follows NCR 4. We ride on cycle paths through the back streets of Richmond, passing Ham House, and continue along the Thames to soak up the ambience. We then return along the riverbanks through a nature reserve, passing historic Teddington Lock to head home through Richmond Park.

LINKS WITH
NCR 4 Thames Cycle Path.

EASY ACCESS
See *www.royalparks.org.uk* for detailed disabled access information with *www.disabledgo.com* link. Surfaces tend to be sandy gravel with some gradients.

PUBLIC TRANSPORT
TRAIN STATION: Richmond Station. Turn **R** just before the bridge to ride to Richmond Station.

PARKING
There are car parks at several of the gates. We've chosen to start the circuit at the Roehampton Gate because this is where the bike hire is located.

BIKE HIRE
RICHMOND PARK CYCLE HIRE
Open every day in high season. In partnership with the Royal Parks.
T 07968 697 541 (Opening hours only)
www.parkcycle.co.uk

BLAZING SADDLES BIKE HIRE
At Richmond Bridge boathouses.
T 0208 948 8240
http://blazingsaddlesbikehire.com

BICYCLE
A local independent bike shop in Richmond, near The Alberts.
T 0208 940 2274
www.bicyclerichmond.co.uk

FOOD AND DRINK
Here along the banks of the Thames, you will find a good selection of eating places including Groucho's, and Stein's Teashop, various pubs and cafes. Go **R** up Water Lane for The Slug and Lettuce.

POINTS OF INTEREST
HAM HOUSE
A unique 17th century Stuart mansion with a sumptuous interior and formal gardens. It is associated with Restoration Court intrigue and Civil War Politics. It is also reputed to be haunted. A restricted number of cycle racks are available within the grounds. *www.nationaltrust.org.uk*

THAMES RIVER BOATS, RICHMOND LANDING STATION
If you fancy seeing London not just from two wheels but from the water as well, why not take a cruise along the Thames to Westminster, Kew or Hampton Court? This company is cyclist-friendly. They will take bikes on board if they're not busy, or you could leave your bicycle chained to the fence by their kiosk.
T 0207 930 2062
Full information on river services and timetables are available from the Transport for London website:
https://tfl.gov.uk/modes/river

FAMILY RIDING
Only if they're road-confident enough to cope with any road sections on links between Richmond Park and the Thames.

S Leave the car park and go **R** on the shared-use sandy path. At the roundabout, turn **L**, following the *Thames Cycle Route NCR 4* sign, to ride on the path beside the road. Cross **L** at the roundabout, still following the NCR 4 sign. Ride up a steady gradient, keeping **SA** where the lane merges into a pedestrian- and cyclist-only stretch passing through a wooden gate.

Pass White Lodge on your left and see Pen Ponds on your far right. It's a far cry from city life. This is perhaps the quietest section of the park: you can hear the grasshoppers!

Leave the traffic-free zone, passing the car park. After the car park, turn **R**, following the white sign *Ham 2 miles/NCR 4*. You are cycling past the Isabella Plantation – we saw some stunning herds of deer basking in sunlight hereabouts. They co-exist well with the cyclists, walkers and cars because, thankfully, most people treat them with respect. At the T-junction, bear **R** on the path. Follow the NCR 4 sign to cross the road and follow the sandy track to Ham Gate.

2 Leave Richmond Park and follow the cycle path (NCR 4) **SA**. Cross at the pedestrian crossing: there's a green bicycle light! Go **SA** then back onto the road at the NCR 4 arrow. Cycle **L** following the tarmac track across Ham Common but, almost immediately at the fork, head diagonally **R** onto the cinder track.

Bear **R** across Ham Common Road and go through the car park opposite, past Avenue Lodge and ride along the wide sandy track. Cross the road and head for Ham House ahead. At the imposing gates, follow the path around the corner.

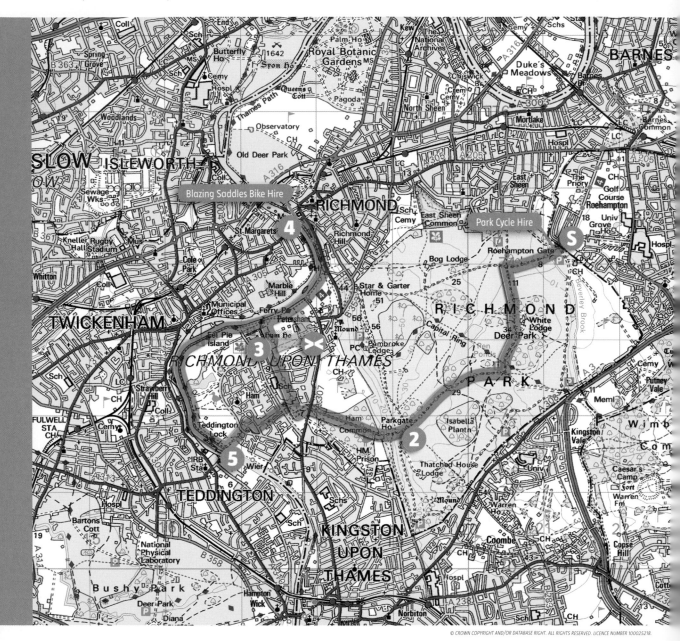

3 Shortly afterwards, turn **L** down the bridleway to join the Thames Path.

OPTIONAL ROUTE

Alternatively, if you wish to see Ham Polo Club, keep cycling, ignoring offshoots to the path. Pass the Ham Polo Club to your left. If you're interested, the club welcomes spectators and picnickers every Sunday from May to September. At the end, emerge on School Drive with care. Before you reach the end of the path, look for a **footpath** going **L** through metal gates and across a drive. **Push** your bike a short distance. At the gate to the Sea Scouts Hut, **push** your bike **L** following the footpath sign to the Thames Path.

When you reach the Thames Path, turn **R** to head into Richmond.

4 Arrive on two wheels along the banks of the Thames in Richmond. There's bags of atmosphere, with boat-builders, buskers and rowing boats. It's an atmospheric location with a holiday feel to it.

Return **L** along the banks of the Thames. Pass the footpath and bridleway to Ham House. Continue on to enjoy a much quieter and more leafy stretch of the Thames. It's funny but as the bird song increases so does the number of pedestrians; perhaps it's the appeal of Ham Lands Nature Reserve. See the Thames Young Mariners Centre. Cycle along this rural stretch of the Thames Path for a while.

5 Reach Teddington Lock. Pass the lock access road on your left. At the blue bridge, follow the white sign **L**, taking the NCR route. Go **SA** on the road to rejoin the path. Cross another road and follow the path. Go **R** and then **L** into Lock Road. Pass Ham Street on your left and keep cycling on Lock Road. Recognise Ham Common with the pond on your right. Turn **R** to rejoin the cinder track across the common and retrace your tyre tracks through Richmond Park.

18 BUSHY PARK

& along the River Thames through Hampton Court Park

CYCLEWAY	COUNTRY PARK	TOURIST TRAIL
GRADE: *		
DISTANCE: 16km / 10 miles		
MAPS: OS Explorer 161; Bushy Park map		

This is a very easy, historic off-road trail, which could be enjoyed by families or couples wanting a leisurely cycle. If you're a tourist, give your feet a rest and soak up some London atmosphere.

Historically, the Thames has always been important so you can sightsee by imagining who has walked or ridden beside the riverbank, and which historic characters have surveyed the same stretch of the Thames as you. Imagine who they were with and what they were talking about...

Hampton Court has seen its fair share of intrigue: being home to monarchs Henry VIII and Charles I, among others, and the home to Oliver Cromwell during his time as Lord Protector of England in the mid 16th century. Cycling along the Thames path beside this palace gives you a real feel for the place and all its history. Finish with a leisurely lunch by the Thames or a look around Hampton Court itself.

LINKS WITH
NCR 4 Thames Cycle Path. Our routes in
Richmond Park (p161, 167).

EASY ACCESS
The paths here are generally firm and level,
both in Bushy Park and along this section
of the Thames. There is disabled access
to toilets in Bushy Park. For a detailed
assessment of surfaces on the Thames Path
between Hampton Court and Kingston
Bridge, visit *thames-landscape-strategy.
org.uk/publications* and browse **Accessible
Thames Walks**.

PUBLIC TRANSPORT
TRAIN STATIONS: **Hampton Wick** (10 mins
walk Hampton Wick gate).
Teddington (10 mins walk Teddington gate).
Kingston (25 mins walk Church Grove gate).
Hampton.
Fulwell.
TUBE: Lots of tube stops nearby.

TO REACH BUSHY PARK
THE STOCKYARD, BUSHY PARK, LONDON
From Hampton Court Road, drive past the
walls of Hampton Court and turn **L** down
Church Grove. Turn **L** into Bushy Park after the
pedestrian crossing. Turn **R**, following signs
for the car park and café.

PARKING
IN BUSHY PARK
The Pheasantry Welcome Centre.
Café, bike racks, toilets.

ALTERNATIVE PARKING
At the Diana Fountain. Refreshments kiosk.

FOOD, DRINK AND ACCOMMODATION
THE PHEASANTRY WELCOME CENTRE CAFE
Next to the parking in Bushy park. Offers
sandwiches, cakes and drinks. Terrace.
T 0300 061 2250
www.royalparks.org.uk/parks/bushy_park

BLUBECKERS RESTAURANT AND BAR
At Hampton Court – just over the road!
T 0208 941 5959
www.hamptoncourt.hcpr.co.uk

CARLTON MITRE HOTEL RIVERSIDE BRASSERIE
The best thing about this place is the terrace
on the banks of the Thames. The food's
not bad either and there are some railings
where you can discreetly chain your bikes.
It's attached to the Carlton Hotel.
T 0208 979 9988
www.carlton.nl/en/hotel-mitre-london

TEMPLEREAD CRUISES
Usually based at Windsor, from where they
run 6 night B&B Thames cruises during
which there are bikes available for your
use. Alternatively, you may take your own.
This independent business is flexible and,
if they're quiet, they're happy to cruise to
requested locations. Best phone for a chat.
T 01332 522 168
www.hotelbarging.co.uk

POINTS OF INTEREST
BUSHY PARK
Bushy Park has long been the playground of
Hampton Court. Cardinal Wolsey gave the
park to Henry VIII and he loved to hunt there.
Oliver Cromwell created the Heron and Leg-
of-Mutton fishponds and, later, Christopher
Wren created two grand avenues. The famous
'Diana' fountain stands at their junction.
In 1830, the park was opened to the public
and Londoners have enjoyed it ever since.
There's an extensive enclosed play area.

The park doesn't encourage or discourage
cycling. There are unmarked sandy shared-
use tracks, but you do need to be considerate
to other users. It's a fantastic place to enjoy
wildlife and you will certainly see Red and/or
Fallow deer grazing. There's a good, fenced
play area which should keep most youngsters
amused for a while.
www.royalparks.org.uk

HAMPTON COURT
This royal palace is perhaps best known for
its maze, but it also offers the opportunity to
explore Henry VIII's Great Hall, experience
the sights and sounds of 'live Tudor cookery'
in the Tudor kitchens, and, the highlight of
many a school trip, the chance to see if those
stories about a ghost in the Gallery are true...
Visit the website for further information
about facilities and exhibitions, historical
re-enactments and family activities.

If you wish to leave your bikes while you look around, use the cycle racks to the left of the main entrance in Tennis Court Lane near the public toilets.
www.hrp.org.uk

COMPANION CYCLING
Companion Cycling is a charity-run scheme which enables people who are unable to ride 'solo' cycles for whatever reason, to enjoy the pleasure of cycling with a companion in the delightful and traffic-free surroundings of Bushy Park.
www.companioncycling.org.uk

THAMES RIVER BOATS
At Richmond Landing Station.
If you fancy seeing London not just from 2 wheels but from the water as well, why not take a cruise along the Thames to Westminster, Kew or Richmond? This company are cyclist-friendly. They will take bikes on board if they're not busy.
T 0207 930 2062
www.wpsa.co.uk

FAMILY RIDING
Yes, with very small children you could stay in Bushy Park. Alternatively, the road link is very short and I would recommend pushing your bikes and using the pedestrian crossing to reach the Thames path.

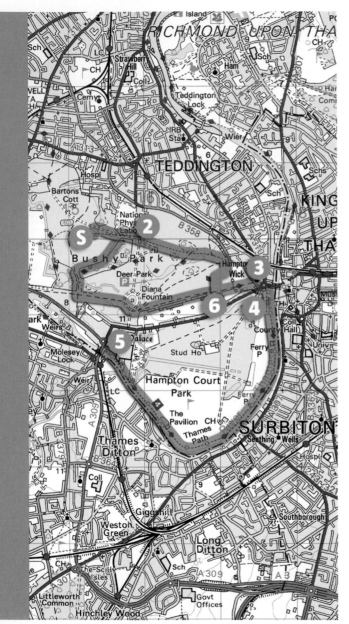

S Turn **R** out of the car park and follow the sandy track opposite. Turn **R** at the road. Cross the road, so that you are on the opposite side to the small gate lodge, and follow the sandy track **SA**. Follow the path to the road.

2 Cross the road and ride along the tarmac track, following the wooden sign for Hampton Wick Gate. This is Cobbler's Walk. Ride along the path through the bracken. Pass Leg-of-Mutton Pond on your right.

At the wooden marker, follow the path round as it curves to the right, ignoring Hampton Wick Gate. Follow the path round the cricket ground. At the far side, turn **L** at the tarmac path.

To continue on a short loop for young families round Bushy Park, turn **R** and go to point 6.

Exit through Church Grove Passage Gate. You may need to push along here when it's busy. Pass the skate park.

3 Families and those who don't like busy roads may prefer to push on this very short road link to the Thames Path. Turn **R** down the B358, passing the play area. Turn **L** onto the A308. If you're pushing there's a handy pedestrian crossing. Turn **R** to follow the A308 towards Kingston and the Thames.

If you wish to follow the Thames Path **L** towards Richmond Park, you will link up with our Richmond Deer Park route (p167).

4 Turn **R** before the bridge to follow the Thames Cycle Path for 3 miles towards Hampton Court and Pier. Please note that **pedestrians have priority along Barge Walk**. Continue riding alongside the Thames as the path turns sandy. Look out for Ravens Ait Island: the location for a recent campaign to have a London 'eco conference centre'. Keep **R** where the track forks to stay on the cycle track.

Pass the gate to the golf course. It is part of Home Park and Hampton Court Palace Grounds. **Please note**, between April and October, there's no access to the formal gardens at Hampton Court Palace via Home Park. Cycle on. There are some out-of-this-world houses on the far side of the river!

Pass through a wooden gate, following NCR 4 signs **SA** and passing The Pavilion. Ride along beside the wall, passing another gate which leads through to the Park.

Cycle alongside Hampton Court. Riding along the Thames Path is a great way to soak up the atmosphere of this historic part of the Thames. Pass Hampton Court Landing Pier where you could hop on a boat trip.

5 You may now wish to have a look round Hampton Court or, to dine, try crossing the road at the pedestrian crossing and you will see The Rivers Edge and Blubeckers.

To return, retrace your tracks along the Thames Path and, at Bushy Park, re-enter through the same gates. Ride **SA** and continue **SA** where the track is joined by the path round the cricket field.

6 Cycle along this easy path. Pass the public toilets and extensive enclosed children's play area with the bike racks handily positioned nearby. Ride on. See the Diana Fountain to your right. She is popularly known as Diana but some think the statue is more likely to represent Arethusa, a water nymph in Greek Mythology.

Cycle past the canal and continue **SA**, keeping the Diana Fountain to your right. Cross the road and continue **SA** on the sandy path opposite. Follow it round to the side of the fountain.

Turn **L** when you reach the tarmac path. Ride **SA**. Notice a brick boundary a little way to your left. Just after it ends, turn **R** down a tarmac path.

Cross the brick bridge and ride on. At the entrance to the Woodland Gardens, go **SA** taking the fork which leads **R**. Where the tarmac path reaches a sandy track and the start of the road, turn **R** into the car park.

19 GUILDFORD
& the River Wey Towpath

CYCLEWAY

GRADE: ✱

DISTANCE: 10.5 km / 6.5 miles to Bramley

MAPS: OS Explorer 145

Cycle alongside the River Wey, through the centre of cathedral city Guildford, and out into the countryside. The River Wey is Surrey's oldest waterway and provides a wildlife corridor while being situated only 20 miles from London. This ride does feel busier than others in this book because at times you can hear the inescapable hum of traffic, but apart from a couple of roads that must be crossed, it's completely traffic-free, and flat too. There's a particular riverside atmosphere to soak up and you see the world from a different perspective when you're cycling by the water. There's definitely something relaxing about it!

Towpath Etiquette: This towpath is not a designated cycle route; parts are quite narrow and sight lines are short. Considerate cycling is permitted along the entire towpath but cyclists must give way to other towpath users and dismount when passing locks and weirs. Some towpaths require a permit. This is free and can be downloaded from **www.waterscape.com.**

surrey & london parks

LINKS WITH
NCR 22. The Downs Link (p152).

EASY ACCESS
Riverside Nature Reserve has a waymarked trail with boardwalks, much of which has access for wheelchairs.

PUBLIC TRANSPORT
TRAIN STATIONS: Guildford, Shalford, Godalming.

PARKING
RIVERSIDE NATURE RESERVE, NORTH EAST GUILDFORD
Turn **L** into Clay Lane from the A3. Turn **L** into Riverside Nature Reserve & Spectrum. Turn **L** down Bowers Lane and **L** towards parking, following the blue bike sign. Turn **R** into Riverside Nature Reserve free car park.
Or turn **R** into Clay Lane from the A3. Park at the Sutherland Memorial Park with playground/toilets. Ride **L** along the A3 on the shared-use cycle path on the pavement. Cross Burpham Lane and bridge over the M25. Turn **L** into Riverside Nature Reserve & Spectrum, and follow the directions above.
www.visitsurrey.com/things-to-do/ riverside-park-nature-reserve-p1162631

GUILDFORD TOWN CENTRE, NEAR ST CATHERINE'S LOCK.
Millbrook Pay & Display car park (£1 on Sun) by the Guildford Boathouse. Turn **L**, push your bike along the main road. Head **L** towards the Hydro Project/council offices. **Push** down the footpath to the **L** of the theatre and go over the Millmead Lock and footbridge to turn **L** onto the towpath.
For more information on Guildford car parks see: *www.guildford.gov.uk/carparks*

BIKE HIRE
If you want to explore on a folding bike, try the Brompton Bike Hire Scheme dock at Guildford Station.
www.bromptonbikehire.com/how-it-works

FOOD, DRINK AND ACCOMODATION
GUILDFORD
Plenty of options.

THE WHITE HOUSE PUB
This Fullers pub is right on the cycleway and has a riverside terrace where you could sit or tie your bikes up.
T 01483 302 006
www.whitehouseguildford.co.uk

THE PARROT INN, SHALFORD
Light and comfortable. Family-owned and family-run. Large terrace where you can keep your bikes safe. Children welcome at lunch and up until 8pm. Six en suite rooms. Lockable bike area for overnight stays.
T 01483 561 400
www.parrotinn.co.uk

BOATING
Guildford boat house no longer offers boat hire. Alternatives below.

Travel the Victorian way with a horse-drawn narrowboat.
www.horseboat.org.uk

FARNCOMBE BOAT HOUSE
Day boat hire
www.farncombeboats.co.uk/dayboats.htm

HOLIDAYS ON THE WEY
www.waterwaysholidays.com

POINTS OF INTEREST
RIVERSIDE NATURE RESERVE
An 80-hectare nature reserve which contains a mosaic of different riverside habitats that support a variety of wildlife. It's popular with birdwatchers, walkers and naturalists, and a waymarked trail has been constructed which includes sections of boardwalk going across wetland and through marshes.

NATIONAL TRUST: RIVER WEY AND GODALMING NAVIGATIONS AND DAPDUNE WHARF
Interactive visitor centre, barge, small shop. River trips on certain days only. NB: There's a bridge across to Dapdune Wharf from the towpath described below so you would either have to lift your bikes across or be happy to leave them padlocked near the bridge.
T 01483 561 389
www.nationaltrust.org.uk

FAMILY RIDING
It's all off-road but you are riding beside deep water. A boathouse owner told me a story about a worried mother whose son turned round to see what she was warning him about and promptly splash-landed in the water. Obviously, it was all the mother's fault... Level, mainly hard-surfaced paths through Guildford but, out of town, some towpaths can be narrow and slippery, especially during or after periods of rain. The section which links with the top of the Downs Link (Broadford–Bramley) is very family-friendly.

S Go through the wooden gate and ride **SA**. Spot the wooden marker post, signed *towpath* and veer **R**. Go through the gates and across the narrow bridge onto the towpath. You are now cycling on National Trust land.

Dismount to cross the bridge. Pass Stoke Lock and ride on. As you approach the bridge, go up to cross the very busy and fast road **with care** (traffic lights further along if you're really stuck). Go **SA** back on to the towpath, following the blue cycle route sign. Pass a small car park area and the Rowbarge pub.

Cross the road, heading **L**. **Push** your bike along the pavement and go across the second bridge. Turn **R** in front of the blue cycle route sign, passing the National Trust River Wey noticeboard. You are now on the left bank. Cycle along the mud track. It can be uneven and narrow in places, leading you unavoidably near the water, but hopefully not into it! Private gardens back on to the towpath each with their own character. Go under a horribly-noisy bridge.

At the next bridge, the towpath continues across the bridge on the opposite bank. Go **R** a short way, **pushing** your bike over the pedestrian crossing to cross the busy dual carriageway. Pass the restaurant and the gym. Cross the road. Turn **R** onto the shared-use wide tarmac path in front of the bridge. Ride through Woodbridge Meadows and see what mythical creatures the tree pirates have sculpted out of felled trees. Spot the tree giant!

Ride on and you will pass another couple of sculptures. Go under the footbridge/railway bridge. (Notice National Trust Dapdune Wharf on the far side.)

This path has a level, easy surface and an urban feel to it. Pass the Odeon Cinema and Costa Coffee: there's a footbridge for caffeine addicts but, once again, lots of steps and nowhere obvious where you'd want to leave your bike.

The path runs alongside the water and this stretch is still easy access. Pass under a metal bridge with ramps which it's easy to rattle up so watch the headroom! Ride on.

Emerge into a car park beside the George Abbott pub. There are bike racks here if you wish to explore the town centre.

Cycle **SA** towards St Nicholas Church and follow the blue NCR sign towards Godalming. Pass the White House pub. Ride through the car park. Pass the Britannia pub (Shepherd Neame). Ride **SA**, **dismounting** at the blue sign.

Push your bike **L** across the footbridge, **ignoring** the blue sign to Godalming which points up Porridge Pot Alley. Go **R** onto the towpath, shortly before Millmead Lock and bridge. In front of the Guildford Boat House, veer **R** and follow the track across the grassy space. There's a large picnic area.

Follow the path **R** at the sluice gate, hence crossing back to the other side of the water. Ride on along this more open, willow-lined stretch.

Pass Ferry Lane. There was a passenger ferry here right up into the 1900's. A Victorian grotto has been built around the natural spring.

Ride on, taking care just after the bridge where there are sandy banks and some significant subsidence. Ride along this bumpy track.

Pass St Catherine's Lock, which is the shallowest lock on the River Wey. You should see a few tugs and canal boats as you pedal along. At Broadford Bridge and the road, turn **L** to go into Shalford, following NCR 22. **Dismount** to go across the bridge.

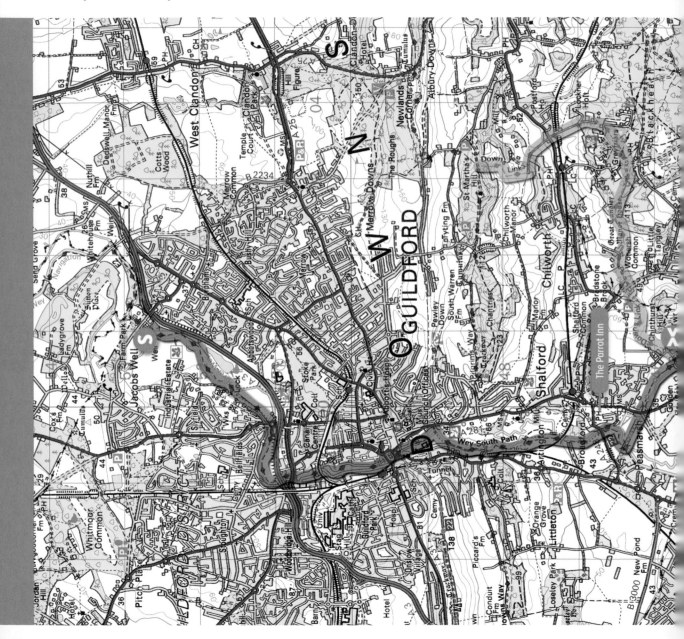

After the bridge turn **R** to go into the Parrot Inn. Turn **L** to join the wooden waymarked signed track for Shalford.

To continue on and connect with the Downs Link, cross the road and continue **SA**, through the wooden gate. Ride on, passing the lock. The path continues towards Godalming. After a short way, reach another wooden gate. Here you must go **R** up the slope and turn **L** to cross the metal bridge, joining the cycleway which links with the Downs Link.

Cross the busy road. Continue **SA**, following NCR 22. From here, it's 6 miles to Cranleigh. You are now riding alongside the Wey and Arun Canal on this hard-surfaced bridleway. This section is a gift and ideal for family riding: it's a hard-surfaced, easy path and you can admire the canal but it's not right next to you.

Pass under the bridge. There's a wooden waymarker. You have now reached Tannery Lane Bridge: see Stage 1 of the Downs Link (p152).

OPTIONAL ROUTE

Turn **L** across Tannery Lane Bridge to reach the most northerly point of the Downs Link, St Martha's Hill, 3¾ miles. This is not an easy option but satisfying if you like off-road climbing and descents.

2 Ride **SA** on the easy-riding track passing beside the site of the Old Wey and Arun Canal towards old Bramley and Wonersh Station. This leads you not only to the delights of Bramley but to the delights of all 37 miles of the entire Downs Link...

20 ALICE HOLT FOREST

FOREST

GRADE: ✳ / ✳ ✳

DISTANCE: Family Cycle Trail: 5km / 3 miles
Easy Access Trail: 2km / 1.5 miles

MAPS: OS Explorer 145; Forestry Commission trail map

Alice Holt Forest offers a family cycle loop and some good opportunities for easy access walking. It's ideal for those who are new to cycling or returning to cycling after a gap, or those who want to combine what's on offer with the other facilities.

It may be disappointing that there's no singletrack, and limited opportunities to expand the family trail, but there's enough here to allow many to sample the great outdoors and relax.

It's a beautiful forest and, if you combine the cycling on offer with the other facilities available, it offers small and large family groups of all ages the chance to plan a day out to match individual needs and wants. The ride is short and the bike hire very convenient so why not mix and match a short cycle ride with time to run free in the play areas, a family barbecue (pre-bookable), high wire forest adventure at Go Ape or a cup of tea at the café?

Alice Holt Forest is situated in the north of the South Downs National Park on the Surrey/Hampshire border. Owned by the Forestry Commission, it is a working woodland and forestry operations may be in progress – keep an eye out for any information signs. As well as waymarked trails, you are welcome to use the many unmarked paths for walking and cycling, but please keep an eye out for other users.

LINKS WITH
NCR 22 – Guildford to Farnham.

Shipwrights Way is almost complete! This new trail is a long-distance path linking Alice Holt Forest with Portsmouth. The name reflects the use of oak grown at Alice Holt Forest for Tudor shipbuilding, linking this site with Portsmouth Historic Dockyard, home of the Mary Rose and HMS Victory. The trail starts at Bentley Station and passes through Queen Elizabeth Country Park. The last section is due for completion in August 2016. For further information see: *http://www3.hants.gov.uk/ shipwrightsway.htm*

EASY ACCESS
Yes, but don't expect completely level, smooth tarmac paths with no gradients! Do expect the chance to experience the forest on firm surfaces, with an off-road feel in conveniently-short loops. Read details of individual trails for more information. A 'Cycling For All' group meets at Alice Holt but this is restricted to committed groups. Adapted bikes are no longer available f or general hire. For further information on how to be involved, see *www.cyclinguk.org/cycle-centre/alice-holt*

HOW TO GET THERE
Alice Holt Forest is 4 miles south of Farnham on the A325. Post code (for Sat Nav) GU10 4LS.

PUBLIC TRANSPORT
TRAIN STATIONS: Bentley (2 miles), Farnham (4 miles). Use Shipwrights Way to cycle from Bentley (2 miles).
BUS: Stagecoach No.18 runs between Aldershot and Haslemere, picking up from Farnham Station and stopping at the Halfway House pub in Bucks Horn Oak (beside Alice Holt Forest).

PARKING
Use one of the two car parks accessed via the main entrance. Parking charges apply.

BIKE HIRE
ALICE HOLT CYCLE CENTRE
Adult and juvenile bikes, tagalongs and trailers.
T 01420 521 297
www.leisurecentre.com/Cycling/ alice-holt-cycle-centre

FOOD AND DRINK
CAFE ON THE GREEN
Offers simple meals, snacks, drinks and ice creams.
T 01420 521 267

Disposable barbecues are forbidden but three freestanding pre-bookable barbecues are available for hire.
T 0300 067 4448

THE CHERRY TREE, ROWLEDGE
Traditional village pub. Hampshire/Surrey border runs through the bar.
T 01252 792 105
http://cherrytreepub.co.uk

POINTS OF INTEREST
ALICE HOLT FOREST
Several decent play areas including Playwood, (for younger ones) Timberline and the 3D maze. Waymarked Walking Trails include the Willows Green Trail (1km), The Habitat Trail with giant play sculptures (1km) and the more muddy, off-road Lodge Pond Trail (4 km). Public toilets, cafe, cycle hire. *www.forestry.gov.uk/aliceholt*

GO APE
High wire forest adventure including high-rise rope bridges, Tarzan swings and zip slides above the forest floor. Minimum age 10 years. Minimum height 1.4m
T 0845 643 2036
www.goape.co.uk

FAMILY RIDING
There's an off-road track through the forest with fairly easy surfaces, and some gradients. Ideal for introducing young families to a short, off-road style circuit.

THE FAMILY CYCLE TRAIL

This firm-surfaced path undulates through the forest. At 3km long, it's manageable by most young families and, in many ways, is more interesting than a completely flat, straight cycleway. They should enjoy the 'downs' but will probably grumble about the 'ups'. There are some well-placed picnic tables though and you can ride it at your own speed, stopping to enjoy the sights and sounds of the forest. It's a great way for a family to explore and a nice way to boost a child's sense of achievement and love of cycling. Older families can ride it faster and argue about who's fittest or fastest...

From the cycle hire entrance, go **L** to take the wide path between the toilets and bike hire building. Lodge Pond Trail leads off to the left and the Family Cycle Trail leads off to the right.

The family trail begins as a narrow-ish gravel path. From the off, you can enjoy a fairly steep downhill which is a great way for the kids to get going, but do keep an eye out for that sharp right-hand bend halfway down the hill.

The surface turns to compacted stone and it can be uneven in places. This path undulates through the forest. The uphills are short, but could be challenging for some children. You could always give them a hand.

There's one rather steep hill but then, at about point 20, the path levels out and widens. It is easier from here on with no more noticeable uphills.

Don't miss the chance to follow the cycle trail **R** off that main path (Old Stagecoach Road) towards Lodge Pond (point 25). Follow the blue off-road trail briefly and you should find both the pond and a picnic table.

Back on Old Stagecoach Road, look out for the view towards the Downs. The path is generally wider now, and the gradients gentler. Ride back past the Education Centre to the bike hire and trail start point.

If you are only looking to do the easiest part of the family circuit, it would be best to start near the Education Centre (point 35) and head for Old Stagecoach Road in an anti-clockwise direction.

EASY ACCESS TRAIL

This trail is suitable for wheelchair and pushchair users. It takes you on a leisurely journey through the forest, enabling many to experience the trees, wildlife and woodland at close quarters. Don't expect a completely smooth and straight tarmac path. It is however firm-surfaced and of reasonable width with some gentle slopes and a mainly even camber.

Look for the large wooden sign in the first car park. The trail leads off from the far side straight into the forest. The first section is even and slightly downhill. There is a picnic table near the first crossroads. The path then climbs in a short, steady up. There's a turn off to the left, which provides a shortcut. This first loop (shortcut via point 6) is probably the easiest part of this circuit in terms of the gradients and camber.

The path is compacted stone and firm. However, from point 3, it does have some slopes, albeit gentle ones. The camber of the path can also be uneven.

Both loops take you through some beautiful parts of the forest.

Key

— — —	Forest path / footpath
	Forest track
⬭	Surfaced path
>>>>	Waymarked route from Bentley Station
⑦	Selected numbered waymarker posts
🏕	Picnic area
🎠	Play area
🌅	Viewpoint
☕	Cafe
🚲	Cycle hire
PH	Pub

0   100   200m

Waymarked trails

Habitat Trail ○ ○ ○
1 km (0.6 miles)
A family walk with
giant play sculptures.

Willows Green Trail ◉ ◉ ◉
1 km (0.5 miles)
An attractive trail with
one steep section and an
optional shorter route.

Easy Access Trail ● ● ●
2 km (1.5 miles)
Suitable for wheelchair
and pushchair users, this
trail takes you through a
variety of woodland and
has an optional shortcut.

Lodge Pond Trail ● ● ●
4 km (2.5 miles)
A more 'off-road' trail to
Lodge pond. Muddy in
places but very beautiful.

Family Cycle Trail ● ● ●
5 km (3 miles)
A relatively easy
ride around the
woods with some
steep hills.

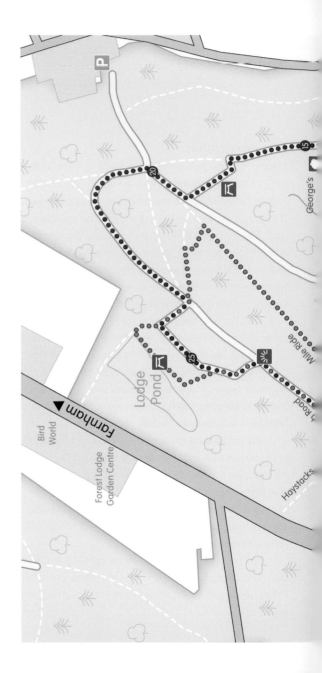

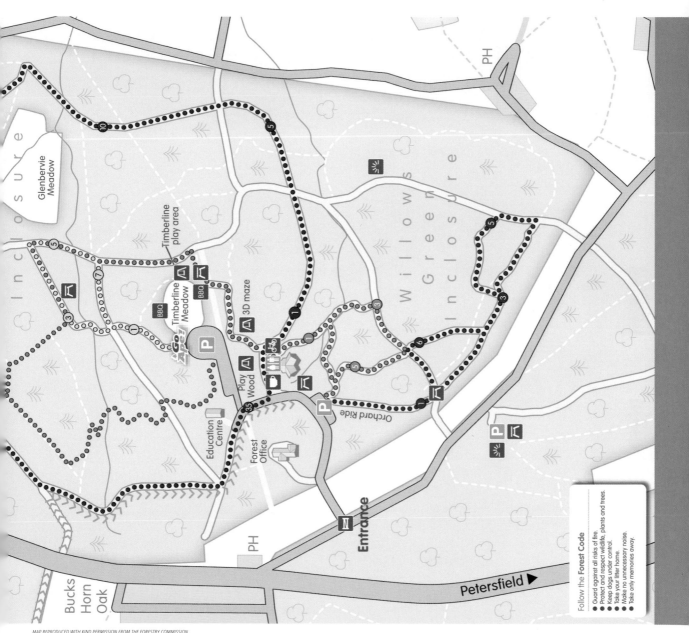

Glenbervie Meadow

Inclosure

Timberline play area

Timberline Meadow

3D maze

BBQ

Play Wood

Education Centre

Forest Office

Willows Greene Inclosure

Orchard Ride

Entrance

PH

Petersfield ▶

Bucks Horn Oak

Follow the **Forest Code**
● Guard against all risks of fire.
● Protect and respect wildlife, plants and trees.
● Keep dogs under control.
● Take your litter home.
● Make no unnecessary noise.
● Take only memories away.

MAP REPRODUCED WITH KIND PERMISSION FROM THE FORESTRY COMMISSION

hampshire

hampshire

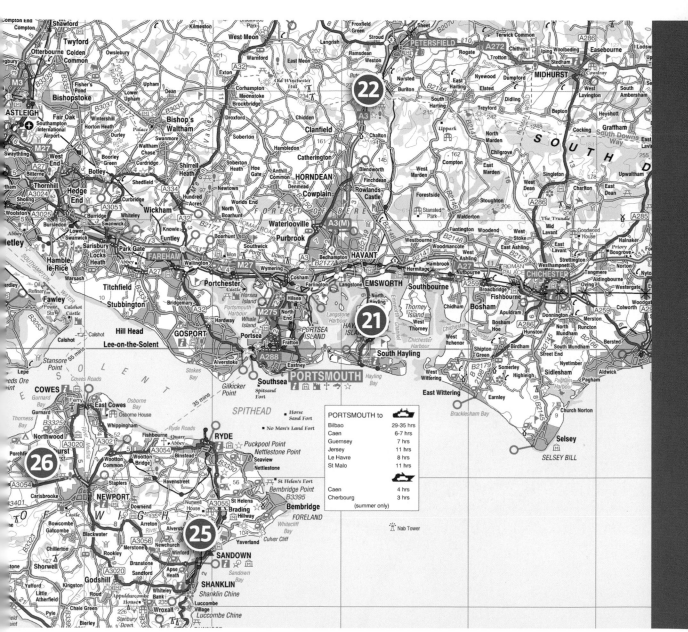

PORTSMOUTH to	
Bilbao	29-35 hrs
Caen	6-7 hrs
Guernsey	7 hrs
Jersey	11 hrs
Le Havre	8 hrs
St Malo	11 hrs
Caen	4 hrs
Cherbourg	3 hrs
(summer only)	

21 HAYLING BILLY LINE

CYCLEWAY

GRADE: *

DISTANCE: 7km / 4.5 miles

MAPS: OS Explorer 120; Hayling Billy Map

This is a short and easy route with the definite advantage of running beside the sea! It's popular with families and cyclists who are looking for a gentle ride. It follows the path of the old Hayling Billy rail line and train enthusiasts can even switch two wheels for steam power once they arrive at the beach! It's a great way to introduce young families to cycling because it's a short, flat ride with the huge reward of a beach and funfair at the end of it. Just make sure they realise that not all cycle rides can lead to beaches and funfairs... The small dirt jump area is a bonus too!

The easiest place to park is at Copse Lane. To make the most of this short trail, we've suggested a round route up to Langstone Bridge before sashaying on down to West Town Beach. This is a permissive path so please be considerate to other users. I wouldn't imagine that it would be a problem: everybody I passed on the trail was smiling. It must be something to do with the rhythm of the waves and the seaside atmosphere.

The Hayling Billy Line forms section 11 of the new long-distance Shipwrights Way.

LINKS WITH
NCR 2 and trail along the seafront.
See *www.cyclehayling.org.uk/the-map/*

Shipwrights Way is a new long-distance trail from Alice Holt Country Park to Portsmouth. The name reflects the use of oak grown at Alice Holt Forest for Tudor shipbuilding, linking this site with Portsmouth Historic Dockyard, home of the Mary Rose and HMS Victory. For further information see: *http://www3. hants.gov.uk/shipwrightsway.htm*

EASY ACCESS
In summer, the surface may be acceptable for some wheelchairs. See the **Access For All** section at *www.conservancy.co.uk* for a short, wheelchair-friendly path at Sandy Point, Hayling Island.

PUBLIC TRANSPORT
TRAIN STATIONS: Havant Park, Portsmouth. PASSENGER FERRY to Portsmouth is currently not running but could reopen. See Shipwrights Way website for alternatives.

PARKING
Driving from Langstone Bridge, pass the petrol station and turn **R** into Victoria Road, where you see the brown sign for the nature reserve. This car park is right on the trail.

FREE CAR PARK IN COPSE LANE
Turn **L** from Havant Road. The car park is opposite a row of terraced houses.

LIMITED PARKING BY LANGSTONE BRIDGE
From the A2053 onto the island, turn **R** into the layby just after the bridge.

IN WEST TOWN
Car park at Sinah Road.
Car park at Beachlands.

BIKE HIRE
BLACK POINT CYCLE HIRE
Located by Sandy Point. They will deliver within a radius of 20 miles.
www.haylingbikehire.co.uk

FOOD AND DRINK
There are a couple of beach snack bars at Beachside. Fish and chips at Eastoke.

ACCOMMODATION
COPSEWOOD HOUSE B&B, COPSE ROAD
Lock-up facilities for bikes, drying room for clothes, children welcome.
T 02392 469 294
www.copsewoodhouse.co.uk

CAMPING
There are plenty of campsites on Hayling Island.

POINTS OF INTEREST
Hayling Beach has a coveted blue flag. West Beach is safest for bathing: see *www.hayling.co.uk* for more information on beaches and Hayling in general.

HAYLING SEASIDE RAILWAY
This narrow gauge steam railway runs every 45 minutes for one mile between the funfair at Beachlands and Eastoke Corner with its shops, pubs and cafes. Members of the East Hayling Light Railway (EHLR) Society help keep this railway running smoothly.
www.haylingrailway.com

FAMILY RIDING
Ideal for an easy family ride!

TO REACH THE START

From the Victoria Road car park, turn **R** onto the trail to reach Langstone Bridge.

From the Copse Lane car park, turn **R** into Copse Lane and then **L** onto the main Havant Road. (Children could push their bikes along the pavement here.) Pass the Yew Tree Pub on your left and turn **R** down quiet Daw Lane. Turn **R** into the next road. At the sharp bend, take the rough track **L**. Stay on this track (ignoring the second track which joins with it). Pass the World War Two Pill House to emerge on the Hayling Billy Coastal Path. Turn **R** to reach Langstone Bridge.

From the layby, cycle through the gap in the wooden fence and follow the trail.

From Beachlands, go **SA** at first roundabout. At the second roundabout, go **L** for Ferry Point. Turn **R** into Staunton Ave.

S You can't go far wrong with this trail as it follows the coastline. To gain the most out of your ride, start by heading **R** towards Langstone Bridge. This far end of the trail is worth experiencing because it runs alongside West Hayling Nature Reserve.

2 The Hayling Billy Line starts beside Langstone Bridge. Langstone Harbour is part of a huge sea water network involving three harbours (Portsmouth, Langstone and Chichester) and the outer Solent. The smell of the sea can be unusually strong hereabouts. This is probably because of the rich organic mud!

It may be muddy but it's also magical because wildfowl and wading birds feed on the food-rich mud. Look out for the ringed plover, wheatear, common sandpiper and whimbrel.

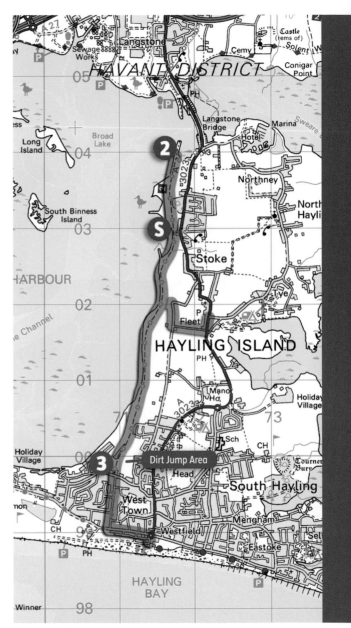

Another plus to the mud here is that whilst it may be smelly, it's out at sea so you don't have to cycle through it... The cycling here is all easy. I guess the only thing that could make it more difficult is the wind.

Cycle south past West Hayling Local Nature Reserve, which does the important job of helping conserve the saline lagoon. This lagoon was created when the old oyster beds were 'made safe' and effectively removed, thereby creating a largely tidal and inaccessible area. Little Terns have been a big success story here: look out for Little Tern Island.

See the Portsmouth skyline in the distance. This path is well-used but has a surprisingly wild feel to it. Probably the sea's influence... Ride past stretches of pebble beach and occasional benches where you could stop to soak up the sea air.

At the World War Two pill box, the path separates into two: take the shared-use path on the **L**.

As well as riding beside the sea, you are also cycling beside meadows. They're not visible because they're under the water but they're there all right and they support three types of sea grass: common, narrow-leaved and dwarf. Seagrass is a marine flowering plant that can live fully immersed in seawater and is nationally scarce. Seagrass provides a 'marine nursery' environment for a variety of wildlife, including cuttlefish, pipefish and the ever-popular seahorse.

Now the trail moves inland.

3 After a while you'll come to Hayling Dirt Jumps. Big and small kids will enjoy this small fenced-off area of dirt jumps, managed by Hayling Dirt Jump User Group.

The trail ends at the former site of Hayling Island Station. The line was in use from 1867–1963. 'Hayling Billy's' were the small engines used to accommodate the weight restrictions of the bridge onto the island.

Emerge at the car park off Sinah Lane.

To take the passenger ferry to Portsmouth, follow the NCR 2 signs.

To continue on to the seafront, turn **L** onto Sinah Lane and immediately **R** into Staunton Avenue. At the end of this straight and easy road, take a **L** for Beachlands or a **R** for Portsmouth via the ferry.

22 QUEEN ELIZABETH COUNTRY PARK

COUNTRY PARK

GRADE: Novice Mountain Bike Trail: ✱ ✱
Advanced Mountain Bike Trail: ✱ ✱ ✱

DISTANCE: Novice Mountain Bike Trail: 6km / 3.7 miles
Advanced Mountain Bike Trail: 5km / 3.1 miles

MAPS: OS Explorer 120; Country Park map: both are sold in the visitor centre.

This is not the place for a family cycle ride with small children as the gradients can be severe and there are few level sections. Paths are not hard-surfaced. These are mountain bike trails and you need a mountain bike to ride them. The gradients mean that the trails are good for fitness training.

The difference between the two trails is not so much in the gradients but more in the width of the path, surface-type and obstacles. In other words, if you're a beginner, it's much easier to stay on your bike on the novice trail.

The trails are short and a good introduction to mountain biking. If your older children or teenagers like a physical challenge and complain that cycle rides are boring, try bringing them here: it's fun. If you're a keen cyclist and you want more of a workout, many opt to ride both trails, some more than once. The park also makes a good starting point for longer rides up into the Downs and Butser Hill. Butser Hill is also part of QECP and a bridleway leads up to the National Nature Reserve near the 270m trig point – the highest point on the South Downs.

Both MTB trails are clearly marked, and maps are available for a few pence in the visitor centre. I've included directions for those who like to know where they're going and what to expect.

hampshire

LINKS WITH
Meon Valley off-road cycle trail: a strenuous 10 mile loop taking in stunning views from Butser Hill.

Shipwrights Way is almost complete! This new trail is a long-distance path linking Alice Holt Forest with Portsmouth. The trail passes through Queen Elizabeth Country Park. The name reflects the use of oak grown at Alice Holt Forest for Tudor shipbuilding, linking this site with Portsmouth Historic Dockyard, home of the Mary Rose and HMS Victory. The last section is due for completion in August 2016. For further information see: *www3.hants.gov.uk/shipwrightsway.htm*

EASY ACCESS
CYCLING FOR ALL
For more information about the inclusive cycling network across the South East, see *www.cyclinguk.org/ride/inclusive-cycling*

TO REACH THE PARK
Queen Elizabeth Country Park is clearly signposted from the A3. Post code (for SAT NAV): PO8 0QE

PUBLIC TRANSPORT
TRAIN STATION: Petersfield station is 5 miles away on the long-distance trail Shipwrights Way.

PARKING
There's a choice of car parks, but you want Gravel Hill. From the main entrance, follow the signs to the *Cycle Car Park* to find Gravel Hill.

BIKE HIRE
No.

FOOD AND DRINK
The café has a large outside terrace and sells snacks such as toasties, baguettes, ploughman sandwiches and so on. There are also kiosks at Juniper play area and the top of Butser Hill.

There are BBQ picnic points at Jupiter and Benham's Bushes in the park so if you come prepared, you could have a BBQ and a bike ride. Pre-booking required.

Tot's Play Trail with wooden play equipment was created by a local sculptor.

POINTS OF INTEREST
QUEEN ELIZABETH COUNTRY PARK
QECP has a large visitor centre, shop (usual souvenirs, local pottery and some handy bike essentials, including helmets), café and toilets.
www.hants.gov.uk/qecp

FAMILY RIDING
Not for young families. Perhaps for older families who like hills.

NOVICE MOUNTAIN BIKE TRAIL

Leave the Gravel Hill car park and follow the **purple** mountain bike signs. Ride a short stretch of park road then follow the trail **R** through a gate onto a mud track. The surface is compacted pebbles and mud, and uneven in places. There's a slight gradient. Veer **L**, following the purple marker. This is a very pleasant wide path, again with an easy surface but slight incline. You won't come off your bike but you will have to keep pedalling. If you're lucky, butterflies will flutter around your tyres to distract you from the gradient.

You may want to push! Turn **R** – the riding is now easier. Turn **L** to head upwards again, following a wide path. Begin this enjoyable descent, although you may feel you deserve to stop and sunbathe at the picnic table at the top. It's a glorious, peaceful spot especially when the sun's shining.

It's a beautiful descent too, the first on a wide steady downhill path. After a while, still descending, the trail veers **L** through the woods on a slightly twisty but easily negotiable path. Even I would have to admit that this descent makes the climbing worthwhile.

Ride **L** and enjoy this downhill along a wide path, cut along the side of the hill. The woods fall away to your right. Rejoin the level path at the bottom of the hill and retrace your earlier tyre tracks. You'll be pleased to hear that it's easier now because you're riding slightly downhill.

ADVANCED MOUNTAIN BIKE TRAIL

From the entrance to the car park at Gravel Hill, cross the tarmac road and find the trail start point. Follow the **orange** bike trail signs. From the visitor centre car park, the trail starts with a strenuous stone and gravel uphill stretch. If you feel like pushing, that's your choice! Soon, the gradient eases off a bit and the path widens. There's a nice downhill stretch. Watch out for the crossroads with footpaths! The path veers off up and **R**, narrowing as it snakes into the woods. There are roots galore, exhilarating sharp turns and bumps.

After a steep downhill, the path emerges onto a wide, grassy track. You can hear, but thankfully not see, the busy Portsmouth-London A3. Ride on up and you'll soon see the track head back **R** into the woods for a gradual, root-laden uphill. It's a relief to see the path widen and the surface flatten, even if you are still heading up.

Enjoy the easy stretch of trail as you pass Beech Hanger. Soon, you veer off into the woods. This trail is made challenging by the gradients, uneven surface and camber of the paths. Next, the path snakes down the side of a hill, like a racetrack if you're my son, or like a place where you squeeze your brakes tight if you're me. There are steep bends and plenty of trees, which you don't want to crash into. The last section of the trail is my favourite: a flinty path through woodland with a steep downhill section at the end.

THE NEW FOREST

FOREST   TOURIST TRAIL

MAPS: OS Explorer 22. Cycling in the New Forest map

In 2005, the New Forest became the first National Park in the South East. It was granted this status because of the extraordinary natural beauty it offers, in habitats as diverse as ancient forest, heathland, bog and unspoilt coastline. There's a lot of history, and a lot of wildlife waiting to be discovered and enjoyed here.

Perhaps best known for the iconic New Forest pony, donkeys, pigs and cattle also roam free as a result of New Forest 'Commoning Rights' and you are likely to come across the pony in particular as you cycle. Please slow down to avoid startling the animals and don't feed them your leftovers!

Roaming by bike is a brilliant way to explore the heart of this National Park, as an extensive on- and off-road network of cycle trails has been created. See the National Park at its best and feel a part of this wonderful forest, but do keep to waymarked paths to help protect this environment. The fact that this haven exists in the frantic South East is brilliant but it will only retain its character if every visitor respects it.

Bear in mind the New Forest is a working forest and any track may be closed for essential repairs or forest operations. In this case, a diversion will be set up and you need to look for the white signs with the green arrows. It's always a good idea to have a map with you just in case of the unexpected!

We offer two very different routes to help you make the most of your time in this stunning area, which offers a vital haven of peace and tranquility in the densely-populated South East.

LINKS WITH
NCR 2.

EASY ACCESS
The New Forest has over 100 miles of trail suitable for those using wheelchairs or buggies. There are waymarked trails at Bolderwood and Knightwood, and disabled facilities at Bolderwood. See *www.thenewforest.co.uk/information/accessible-new-forest.aspx*
  New Forest Park Authority offer inclusive cycling sessions and opportunities for children and adults with disabilities and other challenges. See *www.cyclinguk.org/cycle-centre/new-forest-park-authority*

PUBLIC TRANSPORT
TRAIN STATION: Brockenhurst.

BIKE HIRE
TRAX BIKE HIRE
This company will deliver bikes.
T 01425 618 562 / 07850 043 259
www.bikehirenewforest.co.uk

AA BIKE HIRE, LYNDHURST
ID essential.
T 02380 283 349
www.aabikehirenewforest.co.uk

FOREST LEISURE CYCLING, BURLEY
T 01425 403 584
www.forestleisurecycling.co.uk

CYCLEXPERIENCE, BROCKENHURST
Fast track bike reservations online. A wide choice of bikes including inclusive bikes.
T 01590 624 808
www.newforestcyclehire.co.uk

COUNTRY LANES CYCLE HIRE
In the railway carriage at Brockenhurst Station.
T 01590 622 627
www.countrylanes.co.uk

FOOD AND DRINK
WATERLOO ARMS, PIKES HILL
Just off the A337, nr Lyndhurst. Not directly on the cycle routes but if you're driving home and hungry, this place won't disappoint. Real ales and home-cooked food.
T 02380 282 113
www.waterlooarmsnewforest.co.uk

ACCOMMODATION
CAREY'S MANOR AND SENSPA, BROCKENHURST, NEW FOREST
This independent hotel offers luxury without being pretentious. Cycle breaks which include bike hire are available, or take your own bikes. The car park has CCTV, or there are undercover bike racks by the spa. There's a choice of three restaurants within the hotel: fine dining, French-style or Thai. The hotel has an oxygenated swimming pool with jacuzzi, steam room and sauna.
  For complete rejuvenation, upgrade to use the incredible hydrotherapy complex and range of Thai treatments in the spa.

Hydrotherapy combines exposure to heat and cold and there are suggested programmes to maximise health benefits so you can indulge yourself and feel virtuous about it too.
  Highlights include the storm showers with thunder 'n' lightning effects, scented saunas, ice fountains, heated loungers and fierce water jets in the hydrotherapy pool which target different muscle groups to hit the deepest muscle-knots: Back of the knees? Quads? Great after cycling!
T 01590 623 551
www.careysmanor.com / *www.senspa.co.uk*

BUCKLER'S HARD AND
THE MASTER BUILDER'S HOTEL
On the banks of the Beaulieu River on the edge of the Beaulieu Estate. Bike racks in car park. It should be possible to use the café and toilets at the top without entering, but if you want to explore this tourist attraction, you can pay admission to enter. There's a reconstruction of a master builder's house, a shipwright's cottage and a maritime museum. You can buy tickets for a half hour boat cruise down the river.
www.bucklershard.co.uk

If you just want to walk down to the river, look for The Solent Way footpath where the road turns sharp right. It offers a right of way through Buckler's Hard.

TIP
New Forest cyclist-approved accommodation.
*www.thenewforest.co.uk/cycling/
cyclists-welcome.aspx*

COTTAGES
www.newforestliving.co.uk

CAMPSITES
Camping in the Forest holidays provides ten purpose-built Forestry Commission campsites across the New Forest: Aldridge Hill, Ashurst, Denny Wood, Hollands Wood, Holmsley, Long Beech, Matley Wood, Ocknell, Roundhill and Setthorns. Our routes go directly past Aldridge Hill (need to bring your own toilet) and Roundhill which, in the heart of the New Forest, offers some great walking and cycling opportunities. There're hot showers at Roundhill, plus a choice of wooded or more open pitches.
T 02476 423 008
www.campingintheforest.co.uk

23 AROUND THE NEW FOREST IN 21 MILES

Brockenhurst – Burley – Bolderwood

FOREST

GRADE: ✳ / ✳ ✳

DISTANCE: 34km / 21 miles

MAPS: OS Explorer 22. Cycling in the New Forest map

A 21 mile loop which gives you a good flavour of the New Forest without you ever having to turn your car engine on! The circuit zips through heathland along the *Old Railway Track*, lingers in historic Burley and follows undulating paths up through the forest towards the Bolderwood Deer Sanctuary and the Canadian War Memorial.

But the best is yet to come: a good chance of seeing wild deer followed by a mainly downhill run of forest tracks where the only sound may be your tyres whizzing and leaves rustling. Don't forget to have a quick look at what could be the oldest tree in the New Forest: the Knightwood Oak.

PARKING

Brookley Bridge car park is a mix of short and long stay parking. Public toilets.

ALTERNATIVE PARKING ON ROUTE

Wootton Bridge car park.
Woods Corner car park, Burley.

FOOD AND DRINK

STATION HOUSE BISTRO

This place has a large garden with plenty of bike racks and an undercover area. Its position makes it popular with cyclists and, if you're not in a rush, it's a good place to sit and eat. There's a varied menu of home-cooked food using local, New Forest produce where possible.
T 01425 402 468
www.stationhouseholmsley.com

There's also lots of choice in Burley and Brockenhurst!

POINTS OF INTEREST

BURLEY

Horse drawn carriage rides go from the Queen's Head car park if your legs grow tired!

Podcasts are available from the Forestry Commission on a changing selection of subjects. Download the Forestry Commission New Forest podcasts from
http://tinyurl.com/newforestpodcasts

BOLDERWOOD DEER SANCTUARY

A viewing platform where wild herds of fallow deer may be seen. During summer, the deer are fed between 1.30pm and 2.30pm. Download the 'Guide to the Deer at Bolderwood' podcast from
http://tinyurl.com/newforestpodcasts

THE KNIGHTWOOD OAK

Some say that this is the biggest oak in the New Forest. There's something timeless about trees (perhaps because they often outlast people) and this one's thought to be about 600 years old. It's also rumoured that Henry VIII may have ridden past it when he visited in 1510. Download the Knightwood Oak podcast from
http://tinyurl.com/newforestpodcasts

FAMILY RIDING

The New Forest has a fantastic network of paths ideal for family cycling. However, it also has its share of roads and, in peak season, perhaps more than its fair share of traffic. Out riding, I saw a determined but unsmiling family dragging baby trailers and tag-a-longs up a steep and fumy roadside. It seems a shame for any family outing to be such hard work so where possible we've noted some short stretches and easy parking that should make for a less stressful family outing.

There's limited roadside parking at the start of the *Old Railway Track* – ideal for families with young children who wish to ride a short stretch, avoiding roads completely.

Parking at Burbush Hill is ideal for families wishing to ride the *Old Railway Track* and follow the Trail to have lunch at Station House in Holmsley.

Bolderwood car park has toilets, a field for games and barbecue areas. Why not have a BBQ and do a linear stretch of our trail? If you don't see deer at the viewing point you may well come across them while cycling! Be warned though, the climb to Bolderwood may be a bit too much for little ones.

TO REACH START POINT

From Brookley Bridge car park, turn **L** along Brookley Road. From Brockenhurst Station, turn **L**.

S Outside Cyclexperience bike shop and hire. From the door of the shop, turn **L** and carefully cross the road to ride up Brookley Road with the Foresters Arms on your right.

At the Tudor-style house and the staggered crossroads, turn **L** down Sway Road, taking the B3055 towards Sway. After an easy downhill stretch, pass Brockenhurst Manor Golf Club on your right. Pedal up a short climb, cross the bridge passing over the railway and keep riding. At the T-junction, turn **R**, towards New Milton and Sway. Pass beneath the railway bridge and leave the road at the curve, bearing **R** to follow the *Old Railway Track*.

2 This is the start of the *Old Railway Track*. This wide, sandy compacted-gravel path runs along the line of the old railway track through heathland and is popular with cyclists and walkers alike.

Where the path forks at the wooden gate, go **L** through the wooden posts marked with a green cycling sign. There were several New Forest horses and ponies grazing along this stretch when we rode it and they do make you feel like they're bestowing you with cycling rights rather than somebody giving them grazing rights. Perhaps that's the way it should be?

Ride under several railway bridges and pass through a wild-looking forestry commission campsite. Leave the gravel path, following the grassy green sign. Ride the marked cycle path through the ferns and bracken.

3 Turn **L** onto the road passing Wootton Bridge car park. After the bridge, turn **R** onto the gravel drive, following the cycle path through the wooden gate. You are now riding into Wootton Coppice Enclosure. This gravel path meanders through tall pine trees with some upward gradients. Stop for some water and soak up the peace and quiet.

At marker post 20, you've reached the top! Cycle **R** and keep cycling on this track, following the arrow **SA**.

4 At the very busy A35, cross with care. Go **L** and then immediately **R**. Ride along this narrow but fairly quiet lane which takes you through the Holmsley Enclosure. This lane is enjoyable to cycle because it's downhill but watch out for cars because the lane curves and it is not well-surfaced.

Cycle through the fords and then ride on up the hill on this tree-lined lane. The lane curves at the top. Cycle across the cattle grid and the landscape opens up to give heathland views.

5 ✘ **Optional Route**

If you want to stay off-road and you have time for a leisurely lunch why not go back onto the *Old Railway Track* and head for Station House Café and Restaurant in Holmsley?

To do this, at the bottom of the hill, by the modern building (Holmsley Gate House) turn **R**, back onto the *Old Railway Track*. This track runs through Holmsley Bog and so, not surprisingly, is soon flanked by trees in boggy ground with abundant green undergrowth. Note the old station platform at the end. Go through the gate and you should be able to see Station House opposite, across the road.

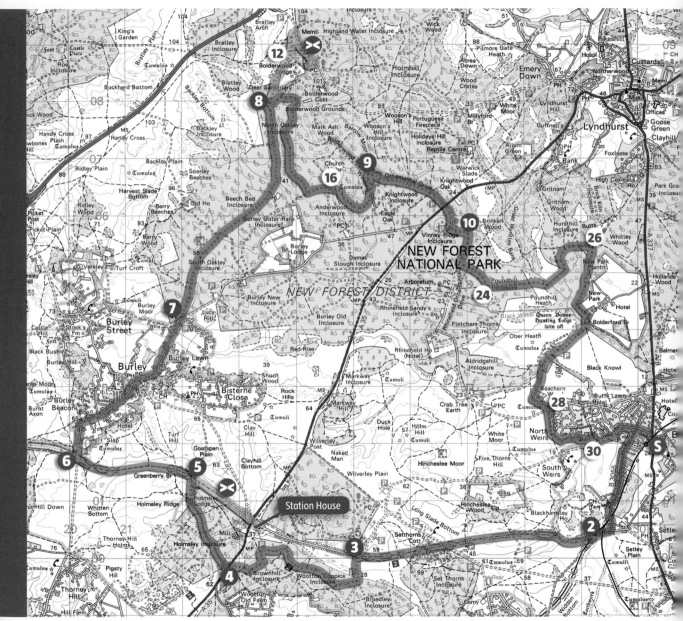

At the modern building, Holmsley Gate House, turn **L**, passing the wooden gate. You are now cycling along the *Old Railway Track* again. At the wooden fence, the track narrows and veers **R**, up onto the old embankment. This track turfs you out at Burbush Hill car park.

6 Cycle **R** on the road into Burley. This road is rather busy but unavoidable if you wish to approach Burley from the railway trail. After the hill, a pavement runs along the far side where families may prefer to cycle. Pass Forest Tea House and Restaurant on your right and climb the hill. This road takes you into the centre of honeypot Burley.

Pass the war memorial and, at the T-junction, turn **R** onto the road – effectively **SA**. You may prefer to walk through the centre of this busy village or stop a while to linger, browse or listen to your podcasts on smuggling and witchcraft in Burley.

At Queen's Head (the same that once had a reputation for smuggling...), go **L** – once again effectively **SA**. Pass the public toilets and car park. Ride on.

7 Turn **L** into Woods Corner Car Park. Cycle past marker post 9. Ride along this forest cycle track for 4 miles through the forest towards Bolderwood. At marker post 11, ride **SA**. Enjoy this surprisingly uncrowded stretch of undulating but not too steep path until you reach the concrete bridge over the stream.

8 **Optional Route to Bolderwood Deer Sanctuary Viewing Point & Canadian War Memorial**

Cycle **SA**. You will see the deer sanctuary on your right, although whether the deer will be visible is another matter. This is a steady climb but it's worth it because the views and the feeling of being at the top of the New Forest will reward you.

Reach Marker Point 12. You are at the top now. Reach the parking at Bolderwood.

If you wish, divert across the road to see the small yet moving Canadian War Memorial. It marks the spot where, up until D-Day, the men of the 3rd Canadian Division Royal Canadian Army Service Corps held their services.

Head **R** down Ornamental Drive towards Bolderwood Arboretum down the hill. Pass the main Bolderwood Car Park with toilets and grassy field on your left. Cycle on down Ornamental Drive. **Dismount** after the cattle grid and go **R** through the gate to the viewing gallery where you may see fallow deer or even unusual white deer. If you don't spot them, don't worry, we were disappointed and then saw plenty whilst cycling the last leg of this loop!

Now you have a choice. I recommend returning downhill to the main route by retracing your tyre tracks to point 8 where you take the **L** fork. Or, for a lazy shortcut on road, turn **R** and head down Ornamental Drive to rejoin the route at point 9. Please note, Ornamental Drive is a small lane through the forest which can be busy and has some winding stretches.

Where the paths fork, turn **R**. At the next fork you must turn **R**. The other path is a footpath but if you want to venture on foot a short distance there's a bench lurking round the corner. Ride on along the bridleway, ignoring all turn-offs. This is one of the quietest tracks we cycled on: peaceful and hardly used. We saw one other cyclist on this stretch.

At the T-junction, turn **L** and, at marker post 16, ride **SA**. Enjoy the downhills on this idyllic forest path. Watch out for the gate on the curving downhill. Keep riding **SA**, ignoring all forks.

9 Turn **R** onto Ornamental Drive. Take care: this single track lane can be busy, although this stretch is straight-ish and not too bad.

At Knightwood, **dismount** and walk a short distance **L** if you wish to see the Knightwood Oak.

Cross the notorious A35 with care to go **SA**, continuing on along Rhinefield Ornamental Drive for a short distance.

10 Turn **L** onto the gravel cycle track through the forest. This next section is great for deer watching! Turn **L** at marker post 24 where tracks cross. Go through the gate into the Wildlife Conservation Area. Look off to the left: you'll see a hide on stilts! If you fancy viewing the deer from it, there will soon be a footpath off to the left. Approach quietly.

Continue on the cycle track, which runs alongside the field of deer so you can view them as you cycle but it seems too easy somehow... Look to the right too. We saw wild red deer in the wild and marshy woodland area to the right too. Pass through the gate and continue riding. Look out for deer leaping from the bracken! Go through another gate, passing marker post 26 to go **SA** and then **R** at the far post signed *Brockenhurst*. Keep riding **SA**.

You're nearly back now. Go through the gate. Turn **R** at marker post 27. Go through another gate and across the bridge.

At the road, at Ober Corner, cycle past Aldridge Hill Campsite and continue **SA**. Turn **R** to use the cycle path to return to the centre of Brockenhurst. Pass Ober Lodge and immediately go **L** on the gravel cycle path. At the road, (marker post 30) go **L**. Ignore 'The Rise' – it goes up! Instead pass St Saviour's Church and go **R** through the ford or across the footbridge. Return along Brookley Road to the bike hire shop, passing Brookley Bridge car park and public toilets on your left.

24 NEW FOREST FAMILY LOOP

plus extension to an off-the-beaten-track pub & the Beaulieu River

FOREST

GRADE: *

DISTANCE: 22.5km / 14 miles (plus 5km / 3 miles)

MAPS: OS Explorer 22. Cycling in the New Forest map

This is a beautiful, easy ride that gives a good flavour of forest and heathland. There's a small extension along quiet lanes to an off-the-beaten-track pub at East Boldre, or you could find somewhere to picnic by Hatchet Pond.

If you fancy a longer ride on some quiet lanes, why not head for Buckler's Hard on the banks of the River Beaulieu. You could have a browse and a cruise down the river before returning to Brockenhurst as dusk falls.

PARKING
From the A337, turn into the forest lane between Balmer Lawn Hotel and the Lymington River. **Ignore** the first car park where children often paddle by the bridge.

PARKING OPTION 1
Tilery Road car park. From here to reach the start, turn **L** out of the car park and cycle along the wide path. Bear **L** at the fork.

PARKING OPTION 2
Standing Hat car park. Ideal for families. Grassy area for picnics and games.

FOOD AND DRINK
THE TURFCUTTERS ARMS
Traditional and atmospheric New Forest pub, off-the-beaten-track. Check website for opening hours as there are no other eating places nearby. B&B available in three self-contained, contemporary apartments in a converted barn at the rear.
T 01590 612 331
www.the-turfcutters-new-forest.co.uk

THE MASTER BUILDER'S HOTEL
T 0844 815 3399
www.themasterbuilders.co.uk

BIKE HIRE AND OUTDOOR ACTIVITIES
New Forest Activities specialise in outdoor activities on the Beaulieu Estate. These include bike hire, bushcraft, archery, canoe and kayak hire.
T 01590 612 377
www.newforestactivities.co.uk

FAMILY RIDING
We wanted to come up with a New Forest loop for families with NO road cycling whatsoever! This is it!

If you want to avoid roads completely you could picnic at Rans Wood car park or cross the B3055 to picnic at Hatchet Pond. You could reach The Turfcutters Arms by pushing your bikes along a very short stretch of B road followed by a small cycle down a quiet country lane.

S Our route starts at Standing Hat car park. Turn **L** and pass through the gate. Take the **R** fork and pedal up the slight incline. At the crossroads (*markerpost 33*) turn **R**. Enjoy the run downhill. Pass through one wooden gate followed shortly afterwards by a second. Ride on.

At the crossroads (*markerpost 38*) go **SA**. Pass through the gate and ride over the railway bridge. Go through the gate at New Copse Cottage. Continue **SA** at the crossroads and pedal hard on this uphill stretch. Look out for ponies!

Pass a cottage on your right. This is a tranquil stretch and we saw deer hereabouts. Keep your eyes peeled...

Cross the road. Cycle **SA**, taking the road into Round Hill Campsite. Pass the campsite reception on your right. At the junction just beyond the hut, turn **R**, following the green markerpost signs to skirt round the edge of the campsite.

At the corner, before you reach the water tower, go **R**, away from the campsite, passing between the green cycle markerpost and wooden gate. Ride along this concrete track through heathland.

2 Keep on this track until you reach the green markerpost at the T-junction. Here you have a choice:

To avoid roads completely, turn **R**. Bear **L**, following the path and green cycle marker post. At another green cycle post, turn **L** towards the road. Cross the busy B3055 road with care.

Go through the gate into Stockley car park. Take the **L** fork. Ride on, staying on this track, ignoring all turn-offs until you reach a triangular T-junction and green markerpost. Go **R**, up the slope.

For a slightly longer ride, with a short but tricky road section, turn **L**.

When you reach the road (B0355), turn **L**. Watch out for traffic and an uneven camber. After a downhill, on the sharp and dangerous bend, you need to look out for a green markerpost on your left and a gate on your right. Go **R**, through the gate and follow the gravel track.

At *markerpost 42*, go **SA**. Stay on this easy cycling path, making the most of the level ground while it lasts. Pedal hard to gain some height. Routes merge on the uphill.

Enjoy the downhill sweep but note the gate at the bottom. Go through, following the green markerpost sign towards Beaulieu. Ride up the grass and gravel path.

3 Emerge at Rans Wood car park and picnic place. Cycle **SA** up the driveway and along what becomes Furzey Lane.

Cross the busy road with care to go **SA**. As you pass Hatchet Pond on your right, turn **L** towards East Boldre. At the junction, cycle **SA** to join the road leading into East Boldre. Pass the Post Office. Look out for the The Turfcutters Arms on your right.

OPTIONAL ROUTE ALONG QUIET LANES TO BUCKLER'S HARD
Turn **R** when you leave the pub. Before St Paul's Church, turn **L** along Cripplegate Lane. Go **L** at the triangular junction, following the white sign towards Buckler's Hard. Cycle on.

Turn **R** onto the road towards Buckler's Hard. Enjoy pedalling along this road. It's wide, not too busy and for some reason, it feels a bit French!

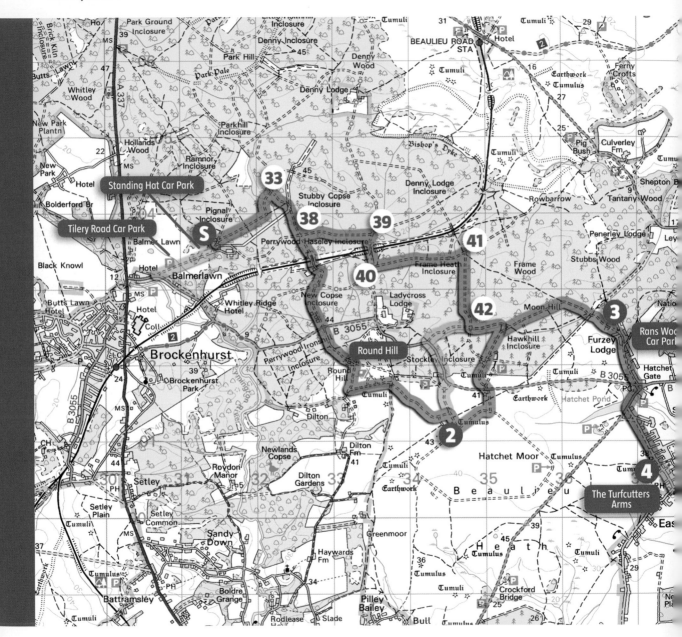

As you come into Buckler's Hard, pass The Master Builder's Hotel on your left. In summer, they hold BBQ evenings overlooking the Beaulieu River. Cycle on. Reach the entrance to Buckler's Hard.

4 After your visit to The Turfcutters Arms and/or Buckler's Hard, you need to return to Rans Wood car park at point 3. The best way to do this is by retracing your tyre tracks. This avoids the busy B3054 into Beaulieu.

At the car park follow the track back towards Brockenhurst. Cycle along this forest track. At the crossroads, go **R** at *markerpost 42*. Go through the gate. This is a deer research area so keep your eyes peeled! At *markerpost 41*, ride **L**. Cycle through the forest. If you're returning late in the day, the forest will reward you by offering some beautiful dusk light and a chorus of birdsong.

At *markerpost 40*, ride **R**. Cross the bridge over the railway and go through the gate. At *markerpost 39*, turn **L**. At *markerpost 38*, cycle **SA**. There's one last hill and a couple of gates to manoeuvre around and, before you know it, you're back in Standing Hat car park.

25 ISLE OF WIGHT The Sunshine Trail

TOURIST TRAIL
GRADE: ✳ / ✳ ✳
DISTANCE: 19.6km / 12 miles
MAPS: OS Explorer OL29; trail postcard

This trail circles an area which boasts the highest sunshine record in the country! It's a favourite of mine because it's virtually all off-road and offers a good variety of cycling while also being suitable for most families with older children. It includes some nice and easy runs on old railway lines, a mixture of rural bridleways and a small-ish section of more challenging mountain bike riding.

The Sunshine Trail offers cyclists the chance to experience a lesser-known side to the Isle of Wight. Ride inland through Alverstone Mead Nature Reserve, a pig farm and the imposing Freemantle Gate. You could call it rural tranquility or rave about the view from the top of a hill but, in the main, it's not the specific things en route which make this trail special, but more the general feeling that you're experiencing something which it might be all too easy to miss!

LINKS WITH
NCR 23, Newport to Sandown cycleway.

EASY ACCESS
The Sunshine Trail isn't, but NCR 23, which runs from West Cowes all the way to Sandown, should be.

PUBLIC TRANSPORT
TRAIN STATIONS: Sandown, Shanklin.

PARKING
Free car park at Sandown Station.

BIKE HIRE
WIGHT CYCLE HIRE, YARMOUTH
Friendly, reliable and convenient cycle hire. Centres in Yarmouth and Brading, and an island-wide delivery service. Make life easy for yourself! This company also provides route information and high quality guided rides with OTC trained instructors off-road or on-road for individuals or groups.
T 01983 761 800
www.wightcyclehire.co.uk

FOOD AND DRINK
If you're taking kids, you would be well advised to take a picnic as eating places are spread out and kids won't be much fun to cycle with if they're hungry!

THE PEDALLERS CAFE
Situated on the trail at Langbridge at Rosemary Cottage B&B. Cycle repair station. Indoor and outdoor seating. Fully licensed.
www.rosemarycottagebreaks.co.uk/cafe.php

THE POINTER INN, NEWCHURCH
Recipient of Island Life magazine's Dining Pub of the Year award more than once for its freshly prepared food, and – more importantly – recommended by locals! Fullers Inn, local ales, small restaurant, cyclist-friendly, beer garden.
T 01983 865 202
www.pointernewchurch.co.uk

THE OLD WORLD TEA ROOM AND GARDENS, GODSHILL
If you fancy a cream tea, Godshill is the place to stop. It's famous for its tea rooms. You can take your pick from several, including the most well known – The Old World Tea Room and Gardens.
T 01983 840 637

There are also several pubs, including the family inn The Griffin
T 01983 840 039
http://thegriffiniow.co.uk
and the 17th century The Taverners
T 01983 840 707
www.thetavernersgodshill.co.uk

ACCOMMODATION
ROSEMARY COTTAGE B&B
Great location with facilities for cyclists, including the use of a large, secure garage for the safe and dry storage of bikes, and facilities for washing down bikes. Utility room is available for drying outdoor clothing, and emergency cycling essentials are available. Cycle hire, repair and rescue, and luggage transfer can also be arranged.
T 01983 867 735
www.rosemarycottagebreaks.co.uk

GODSHILL PARK FARM HOUSE
Offers 3 self-catering cottages and luxury B&B.
T 01983 840 781
www.godshillparkfarm.uk.com

ISLE OF WIGHT CAMPER VAN HOLIDAYS
Hire a camper van to tour and camp the island in style. They can supply bike racks on the campers at no extra cost and will arrange bike hire. Bikes can either be ready and waiting on your camper van or delivered to a chosen campsite.
T 01983 852 089
www.isleofwightcampers.co.uk

WIGHT LOCATIONS
No specialist facilities for cyclists but this small agency will give you friendly advice and share local knowledge so that you can choose a holiday cottage in the right location for you.
T 01983 811 418
www.wightlocations.co.uk

POINTS OF INTEREST

ALVERSTONE MEAD NATURE RESERVE

There are some interesting habitats here, well worth preserving since 95% of Britain's lowland wetland grassland has disappeared since World War Two. Some water meadows beside the River Yar are a Site of Importance for Nature Conservation (SINC), with scarce and interesting wetland flower species and invertebrates, especially dragonflies. The meadows, with their old ditch drainage systems, are hunted by barn owls, kingfishers and herons, with other wintering wildfowl, for example snipe and teal. Wight Nature Fund hopes to preserve and enhance the wildlife of these meadows by careful control of water levels, combined with traditional, chemical-free summer grazing by farm animals. Volunteers remove willow to keep the wet meadows' open aspect for wetland flora and water voles.
http://www.wightnaturefund.org.uk/ Alverstone%20Mead

SPOTTING SHY WATER VOLES

If you're here on a windless day, and you keep very quiet, you might be lucky enough to spot a water vole. Listen for a sound which sounds like somebody munching crisps followed by a plop as they slip into the water. You'll know they're there somewhere...
Failing water voles, why not see how many different dragonflies you can see? And you certainly won't miss the distinctive cows!

APPULDURCOMBE HOUSE AND THE FREEMANTLE GATE

The partially-ruined Appuldurcombe House stands in grounds designed by Capability Brown. The English Baroque style house was once the grandest and most striking house on the Isle of Wight. Since then, it has been used as a hotel, a college for young gentleman, a home for monks and a base for troops in the First and Second Wars. Damaged by a mine in 1943, the house is now a shell. The ruins are under the guardianship of English Heritage and open to visitors.

Freemantle Lodge Gateway was built in the late 19th century and formed part of Appuldurcombe Park. This open parkland was planted with scattered trees and woodland, plus more unusual features, including a ha ha and fountains, built during the 1830s. The two gatehouses were built slightly later. *www.english-heritage.org.uk/visit/places/ appuldurcombe-house/*

FAMILY RIDING

The great thing about this loop is that it's almost all off-road, which is quite unusual for a trail this length that's manageable for a family. It's not an easy ride because, while mainly flat, there are some gradients and a mix of surfaces but, for an older family, it's a good challenge and a beautiful way to see this island.

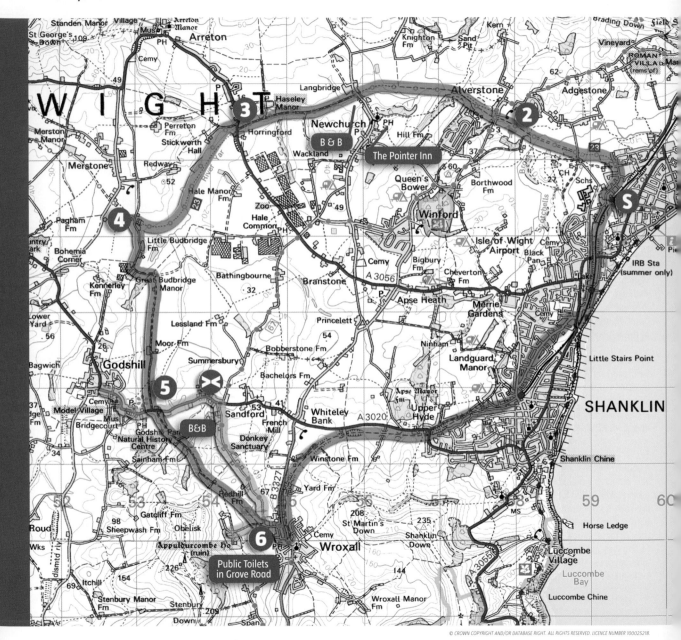

S Sandown Station is the official start. Leave the car park via the main entrance and follow the blue Sunshine Trail signs **R**. Ride down the hill along Simeon Path. Very soon, turn **R** along the tarmac path. Follow the path **R** in front of the metal gate, going through the underpass beneath the railway. You are following signs for the Sunshine Trail and Newport NCR 23.

Turn **R** along Perowne Way, cycling on the road. There is pavement alongside. Follow the road round. Just after the Fairway Holiday Park, turn **L**, following the blue Sunshine Trail sign.

Ride along this tarmac cycleway. Take care at the white gates: here a road crosses the cycleway. The island's cycleways are a far-sighted resource, which enable people to explore the island in a way that is both good for the environment and good for you! Please remember it's a shared-use path and be considerate in how you ride.

Cycle on towards Newport, enjoying views over farmland.

2 The cycleway takes you through Alverstone Mead Nature Reserve and there's a lot to see if you look carefully. Stop at the 'Wetland Walk' if you wish. A river runs parallel to the path and there are some patches of ancient woodland, known locally as Borthwood Lynch Wetland.

At Alverstone, give way to cross the road at the white gates. Continue riding **SA** towards Newport. Pass the Mill and ride on. Keep **SA** on this pleasant, easy-to-ride cycleway through Wight Countryside.

Go through the wooden gate. The path narrows and you reach a fairly busy road. Go through the white gates and turn **L**.

Head diagonally **L** across the road to ride on the cycleway **SA**, following signs for NCR 23. Pass Rosemary Cottage B&B, then a lake on your left.

3 You will reach a main road (A3056 at Horringford Bridge). Turn **R** to use the controlled crossing. (Ever seen a separate horse crossing?)

To explore Arreton Village, turn **R**.

To continue on the Sunshine Trail, go **L** down the public bridleway which forms part of the Newport-Sandown cycleway. At the white gate, veer **L** towards Newport, following NCR 23. Ride on.

Cross the wooden bridge where you are advised to **dismount** as it becomes slippery when wet. This long, wide bridge wends its way over wet ground. At the end, the cycleway leads you **R**. Follow NCR 23 signs and look out for sparrowhawks too! Pedal hard on the slight uphill section.

4 Go under a brick bridge and, almost immediately, turn **L**, doubling back on yourself. You are heading towards Godshill.

Turn **R** along the lane for Godshill. Pass Merstone Fisheries. The path stays wide but becomes rougher. Look out for the blue Sunshine Trail sign before the glasshouses.

Head **L** along the mud track, passing in front of Burbridge Manor. Keep riding **SA**, following the signed bridleways through the fields. You will see an outline of a church on the right. Pass beside a pig farm – you can't miss it! You might see piglets if you're lucky. This stretch can be muddy. Ride through the buildings, keeping **SA**. Cycle on.

hampshire

5 At the road, by the entrance to Moor Farm, you have a choice:

Ride **R** to detour into the picturesque cream tea haven of Godshill.

Ride **SA** onto the bridleway almost opposite for the 'challenging off-road mountain bike section'. It is steep, and it's muddy but there are some beautiful views to be savoured at the top.

✂ Ride **L** for the road alternative, but these aren't quiet roads and there's a fair bit of traffic so it's not necessarily the easier option. Ride up Shanklin Road. Turn **R** into Park Hill Farm and re-join the main route at point 6 below.

To follow the mountain bike trail, cross the road diagonally (going **L** and then immediately **R**), to ride **SA** up the bridleway, following the Sunshine Trail signs. Pass Godshill Park Farm House. Ride with the stone wall on your right, keeping **SA**, passing through the gate to follow the Lakeview and the Sunshine Trail.

Climb the hill! It's a big hill which some people won't like! At the top, keep **SA**, going through the side gate on the huge, imposing Freemantle Gate.

After the gate, the temptation is to ride full steam ahead on the obvious and easy path but it's actually a footpath. Instead, at the tall metal markerpost you will soon see, leave your path to head **L** across the grass on the bridleway. Follow this undulating track as you bump your way down over the grass and towards Wroxhall.

Go through the gate and turn **L**. At the road, turn **R**.

6 **Push** your bike a short distance up the tarmac footpath to detour to English Heritage.

Ride up and into the village. At the main road, the Sunshine Trail is clearly signed to the **R**. St John's Road is a busy stretch of road and uphill too. You may want to push on the pavement. After the church, turn **L** into Station Road and **L** again into Station Road, following the blue Sunshine Trail signs!

When you're almost at the top of the hill, turn **L** into Yarborough Road. At the bottom of the hill, turn **L**, following the blue Sunshine Trail signs. Cut through between the houses and turn **R** onto the narrow, stony bridleway. The track broadens out and runs along the top of an old embankment. Follow this track to Shanklin. Pass through several bridges on this easy-cycling, old railway track. Watch out for hanging brambles!

Emerge on the drive to Lower Hyde Holiday Park. Ride **SA**. At the busy road, turn **L**, and keep following Sunshine Trail signs. After a short distance, turn **R** along Green Lane. It's a nasty turn!

Ride to the end of Cemetery Road. Cross Sandown Road, using the nearby crossing if necessary.

Ride **SA**, following the gravel track signed *Sunshine Trail*. Use the railway crossing with care: fast frequent trains! Ride **L**, following the blue signs. Follow the path which exits Cliff Gardens and runs beside the railway line. Pass the entrance to Lake Station.

Ride to the T-junction at the end of Brownlow Road, turn **L** and then immediately **R**, following the blue Sunshine Trail signs. Ride up the short, steep slope of The Mall. Turn **L** into the park entrance. Ride **SA**, across the grass, keeping parallel with the railway.

Exit through the metal gates. Don't go through the underpass unless you want to do the whole ride again! Ride **SA** and back into the car park!

26 THE MEDINA CYCLEWAY
& Parkhurst Forest

FOREST	CYCLEWAY
GRADE: ✳ / ✳ ✳	
DISTANCE: 15km / 9.3 miles	
MAPS: OS Explorer 29; Red squirrel safari postcard	

I came up with this loop when I was looking for a satisfying but relatively short off-road circuit to ride with my family. It starts on the cycleway, which runs from Cowes to Newport beside the Medina Estuary, and veers off and up into Parkhurst Forest. You do have to climb, but mainly on hard surfaces, which means the forest section is almost all downhill and, guess what? You can't beat going downhill through a forest!

When we were riding this route, we discovered that there are plans afoot to develop Stag Lane in terms of junctions and a cycle path so I would imagine that this trail will only become easier to ride over time.

I've kept the route through the forest as simple as I can because it's easy to get confused on the maze of unmarked paths. The forest tracks are nearly all mud, with surfaces which vary depending on the weather. The adventurous and energetic may want to venture further into the forest in the hope of finding the red squirrel hide!

LINKS WITH
Cowes – Newport – Sandown Cycleways.

Catamaran/ferry links to Southhampton join NCR 23 to West Cowes. On via Newport to Sandown.

Catamaran/ferry links to Lymington/Portsmouth.

EASY ACCESS
The Cowes-Newport Medina Cycleway is hard-surfaced and should be easy access. There's a slight slope at the Cowes access point. Only one road in the forest is hard-surfaced. There is access to the squirrel hide in Parkhurst Forest for some wheelchair users, but access is via gravel paths.
www.gifttonature.org.uk

DEVELOPMENT
Plans to improve the Medina Cycleway include lighting. Also, on Stag Lane, plans for a cycle path, safety barriers at junctions with the Medina Cycleway and an improved junction with the A3020.

PARKING
SOMERTON PARK AND RIDE
Long stay car park by the roundabout on the way into Cowes from Newport on the A3020.

COWES
Limited roadside parking at start of cycleway in Cowes.

PARKHURST FOREST
Alternative start point and car park in Parkhurst Forest.

BIKE HIRE
WIGHT CYCLE HIRE, YARMOUTH
Friendly, reliable and convenient cycle hire. Centres in Yarmouth and Brading, and an island-wide delivery service. Make life easy for yourself! This company also provides route information and high quality guided rides with OTC trained instructors off-road or on-road for individuals or groups.
T 01983 761 800
www.wightcyclehire.co.uk

TOP GEAR VEHICLE RENTALS, COWES/SANDOWN
T 01983 400 055 (Sandown) / 01983 299 056 (Cowes)
www.isleofwighthire.co.uk

FOOD AND DRINK
Lots of choice of places to eat in Cowes, including:

SAILS CAFÉ, SHOOTERS HILL
Let the food at this café surprise you! Simple, good value and delicious home-made food. Baguettes, paninis, mezza lunas, toasted bagels, jackets, salad bowls. Sails will also do packed lunches to order.
T 01983 289 758
E *enquiries@sailscafe.co.uk*

Or stop for a picnic in Parkhurst Forest.

POINTS OF INTEREST
ISLE OF WIGHT CYCLING FESTIVAL
This annual, week-long cycling event has a huge variety of cycling activities on offer. There are options for all cyclists from families to infrequent riders, from new enthusiasts to the super-fit.
www.sunseaandcycling.com

RED SQUIRRELS
The Isle of Wight supports the largest population of red squirrels in southern England, and it's an important habitat. There are only about 160,000 red squirrels left in the UK, compared to 2.5 million greys. The Solent forms a natural barrier to keep the grey squirrel at bay and it's vitally important that the red squirrel's island habitats are preserved.

RED SQUIRREL VIEWING HIDE

Red squirrels are elusive creatures and are not easy to spot. The red squirrel viewing hide at Parkhurst Forest is a Gift to Nature Project and offers locals and visitors a greater chance of seeing these creatures. To find it, follow the squirrel safari signs, and/or look to see where it's marked on our map.
www.gifttonature.org.uk

PARKHURST FOREST

Parkhurst Forest is made up of ancient woodland (planted pre-1600) and plantation woodland. It is partly a Site of Special Scientific Interest. Interesting or rare species in residence include Pearl-Bordered Fritillary butterflies, White Admiral butterflies, long-eared owls and great crested newts.

FAMILY RIDING

This is a great ride for families who want to venture off the cycleways and explore without going too far. Road links are tricky but short and, where busy, there are cycle paths or pavements young children could push along, and traffic lights or underpasses which will help you all cross safely.

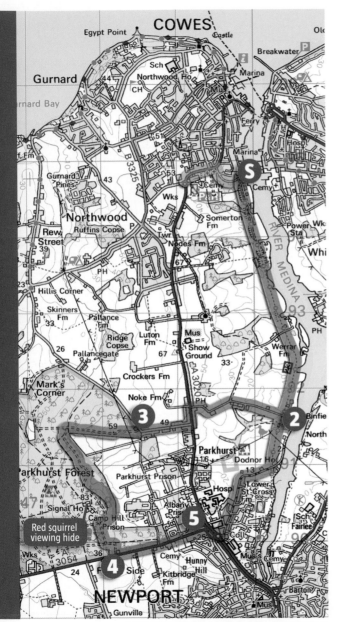

TO REACH THE START FROM COWES TOWN CENTRE

Cycle along Arctic Road, following signs for NCR 23 towards Newport. At the end turn **R** at the mini roundabout. The cycleway is on your left.

TO REACH THE START FROM SOMERTON CAR PARK

Turn **R** out of car park. **Push your bike** on the pavement to avoid the busy roundabout. Cycle down the hill, passing a fishing lake on your right. Go past Cowes Medical Centre. Continue down Newport Road, passing the cemetery. Turn **R** into Arctic Road, following the blue cycleway sign.

S Turn **R** to join the cycleway. Pass beside the gate and you should be able to see the River Medina on your left. Ride on, enjoying this off-road, easy-to-ride, hard-surfaced track.

2 At the road opposite the metal gates, labelled *Sir Robert McAlpine*, turn **R**. This is Stag Lane. It's a wide, industrial road with infrequent traffic. It's something of a climb then it levels out. Pass a fishing lake on your left. Keep climbing and just think, at least it means you won't have to climb much on the rough tracks in the forest. Keep pedalling past Staghorn Motors and follow the road around as it curves. As you reach the A3020, you'll see The Old Stag Inn on the corner.

Turn **L** onto Horsebridge Hill at the traffic lights. This is a busy road but there is currently a pavement where you could push for this short stretch. I believe a cycle path is planned.

Turn **R** into Noke Common, pushing across the pedestrian crossing. Pedal hard to conquer one last short climb. Near the top of the hill, there's an interesting view looking down over the prisons to your left.

3 Where Noke Common Road curves, turn **L** into Forestry Commission-owned Parkhurst Forest. Be aware: this is a working forest. This is Noke Gate Entrance. Go past Noke Gate Lodge, round the wooden gate and cycle up a slight gradient along this leafy, wide conglomerate track. Make the most of this fast, forest downhill run!

At the bottom, turn **L**, past the small wooden fence posts.

To explore the forest further you could try going **SA**. If you turn **L** at some point, and ride down through the forest you would eventually reach Forest Road.

The forest tracks are unmarked and for cyclists who don't want to run the risk of too much extra cycling or who have tired children in tow, I've kept it very simple.

Stay on this path as it curves and climbs through the edge of the forest. Don't worry, after the climb, there's a lovely long downhill. Eventually, after a very small up, you will hit a tarmac road.

Turn **L** into Signal Drive to exit the forest via the main entrance. Pass the car park (picnic tables) on your right and follow the road round to your **L** down the slope. The drive curves to the right and reaches a busy road.

4 Turn **L** onto Forest Drive. This is the longest road section and it's not ideal: young children may want to push their bikes along the pavement. Pass the school on your right and continue until you reach the roundabout at the end.

5 This is a horribly-busy junction best negotiated in the following way:

Push your bike along the pavement to the right. Head towards the second roundabout. At the second roundabout, cross the road, heading towards the HSS Hire Shop and bus stop. Go through the underpass which leads off beside the hedge. Emerge at B&Q. Go **L**.

Go round the roundabout. Take the second exit towards the industrial estates. Pass the hospital on your left. Turn **R** into Dodnor Lane. **Ignore** the right turn into Dodnor Mews which leads to the cycleway into Newport.

Ride down the lane, passing various houses. Pass the stables at Dodnor Manor Farm. At the red and blue road signs, turn **L**. You are back on the Medina Cycleway!

Ride on, cycling across the unexpected and in its own small way, spectacular, bridge over Parkhurst Stream. Enjoy the easy ride back into Cowes and look out for red squirrels foraging. Dusk and dawn are reputedly particularly good times for spotting them along this cycleway!

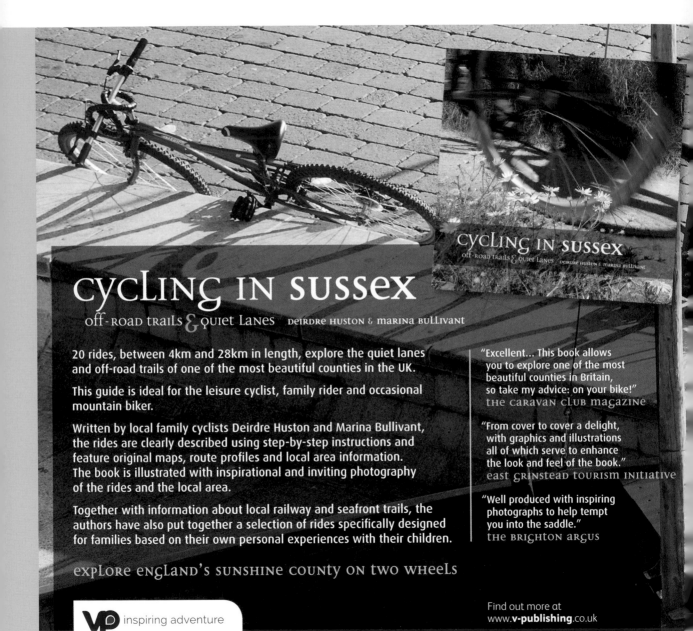

cycling in sussex

off-road trails & quiet lanes — deirdre huston & marina bullivant

20 rides, between 4km and 28km in length, explore the quiet lanes and off-road trails of one of the most beautiful counties in the UK.

This guide is ideal for the leisure cyclist, family rider and occasional mountain biker.

Written by local family cyclists Deirdre Huston and Marina Bullivant, the rides are clearly described using step-by-step instructions and feature original maps, route profiles and local area information. The book is illustrated with inspirational and inviting photography of the rides and the local area.

Together with information about local railway and seafront trails, the authors have also put together a selection of rides specifically designed for families based on their own personal experiences with their children.

explore england's sunshine county on two wheels

"Excellent... This book allows you to explore one of the most beautiful counties in Britain, so take my advice: on your bike!"
the caravan club magazine

"From cover to cover a delight, with graphics and illustrations all of which serve to enhance the look and feel of the book."
east grinstead tourism initiative

"Well produced with inspiring photographs to help tempt you into the saddle."
the brighton argus

vp inspiring adventure

Find out more at
www.v-publishing.co.uk

MountainBiking
in South East England

South East Mountain Biking North & South Downs is a compact guide to the best riding on the Downs of Kent and Sussex. The area is criss-crossed with bridleways and byways – escape the towns and cities and explore the finest woodland and open chalk tracks while enjoying panoramic views of the Weald and the English Channel.

South East Mountain Biking Ridgeway & Chilterns takes in the best riding either side of the ancient Ridgeway and the Chiltern Hills west of London. Explore the Thames Valley, the Hampshire Downs and lose yourself in the Chilterns.

Each guide offers 24 routes suitable for riders of all abilities and features easy-to-follow directions as well as details of distance, grade of difficulty, route profiles and local area information including refreshment stops.

Guidebooks from Vertebrate Publishing

Find out more at www.**v-publishing**.co.uk

 inspiring adventure

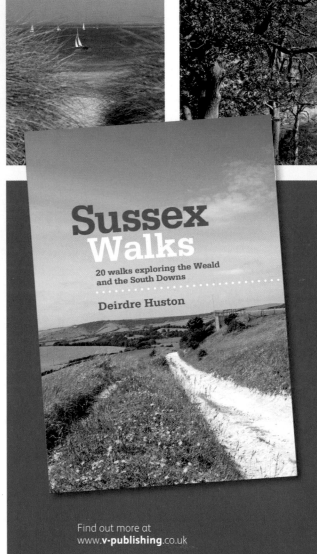

Sussex
Walks

20 walks exploring the Weald
and the South Downs

Deirdre Huston

Sussex
Walks

20 walks exploring the Weald and the South Downs

Sussex Walks by Deirdre Huston is a collection of 20 circular walks, between 3.5 and 12 miles (5 and 19 kilometres) in length that explore the length and breadth of the county of Sussex.

Each walk features:

- clear and easy-to-use **Ordnance Survey** 1:25,000 maps
- easy-to-follow directions
- information on local history, wildlife, refreshments and terrain.

Map data

Find out more at
www.**v-publishing**.co.uk

VP inspiring adventure

Day Walks on the SouthDowns

20 Circular Walks in South East England

Written by **Deirdre Huston**

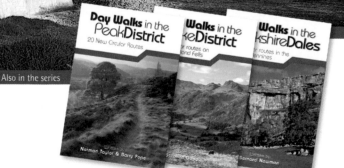

Also in the series

Vertebrate Publishing's Day Walks guidebooks
are written by local hill walkers and feature:

» 20 day-length walks
» **Ordnance Survey** 1:25,000 maps
» easy-to-follow directions
» distance and navigation information
» refreshment stops and local information.

Find out more at www.**v-publishing**.co.uk

 inspiring adventure

vp
inspiring adventure

At **Vertebrate Publishing** we publish books to inspire adventure.

It's our rule that the only books we publish are those that we'd want to read or use ourselves. We endeavour to bring you beautiful books that stand the test of time and that you'll be proud to have on your bookshelf for years to come. The Peak District was the inspiration behind our first books. Our offices are situated on its doorstep, minutes away from world-class climbing, biking and hill walking. We're driven by our own passion for the outdoors, for exploration, and for the natural world; it's this passion that we want to share with our readers.

We aim to inspire everyone to get out there. We want to connect readers – young and old – with the outdoors and the positive impact it can have on well-being. We think it's particularly important that young people get outside and explore the natural world, something we support through our publishing programme.

As well as publishing award-winning new books, we're working to make available many out-of-print classics in both print and digital formats. These are stories that we believe are unique and significant; we want to make sure that they continue to be shared and enjoyed.

For more information about **Vertebrate Publishing** please visit our website: **www.v-publishing.co.uk** or email us: **info@v-publishing.co.uk**

Photo: John Coefield